"*The Reflective Administrator: A Leader-Centered Focus* is an essential resource for leaders desiring to gain a deeper knowledge of reflection as a professional tool. This book challenges leaders to embrace going against the status quo and incorporate a rewarding change agent mindset. The authors do a great job of drawing the readers in with an easy to read and supportive framework, case studies, and examples of reflective learning. I was so inspired after reading this book that I personally challenged myself to becoming more reflective within my personal and professional life. If you are looking for an insightful, practical, implement ready, and life changing book to improve your entire life I highly recommend this one whole-heartedly!"

Eva Carleen Alexander, *EdD, Adult Education Adjunct Instructor, Northshore Technical Community College*

"The importance of intentional reflective practice cannot be overestimated. *The Reflective Administrator* moves from theory and research through practical application including cognition and feelings in reflective practice. The inclusion of 'Mirror Moments' gives the study of becoming a reflective administrator a very practical and helpful component that one can immediately incorporate into practice. Connecting mindfulness and reflective practice is another practical gem incorporated in this text. This book is useful for not only public administrators but for any leader interested in becoming more reflective in their career path or practice."

Joyce Jemison, *Licensed Speech and Language Pathologist, USA*

"*The Reflective Administrator: A Leader-Centered Focus* is not only a must-read, it is a must-do! As a professor who teaches working professionals in leadership positions in organizations of all types to practice applied leadership, this book is filled with excellent theoretical foundations, research and practical case studies that my students can use. It is also essential to administrators in any field as a treatise for reflective practice. The text builds depth and breadth of understanding from the first chapter through the last and concludes with a crescendo...by framing reflection as forethought. Simply brilliant! I cannot recommend this book enough."

Jeni McRay, *PhD, Associate Professor of Leadership Studies, Assistant Provost of Internationalization & Strategic Initiatives, Fort Hays State University*

"*The Reflective Administrator: A Leader-Centered Focus* eloquently conveys a fresh perspective on well-known theories germane to reflective thought and presents practical ways to employ reflection within the public sector classroom and workplace. The book effectively guides readers through relevant reflective thought theories, the usefulness of reflection in the workplace and wisely incorporates practical case studies for further reflection and study. This influential book focuses on how to apply reflection in public service fields, describes how civil service professionals can incorporate reflective practice to develop a personal ethical framework, and inspires readers to integrate reflective thought into their leadership toolkit. The book earns my highest recommendation and inspires me to encourage others to add this gem to their professional development library."

David Ximenez, *Associate Vice Chancellor, Enrollment and Academic Support Services, Tarrant County College District*

THE REFLECTIVE ADMINISTRATOR

The Reflective Administrator takes the well-grounded theories of reflective thought out of the classroom setting and delivers them into the public sector workplace.

The intentional practice of reflection is useful not only with regard to experiential learning in public administration education but also within the profession itself. The text dispels misconceptions about what reflective practice entails and offers the reader practical tools to implement in both the classroom and professional environments. The book begins by walking the reader through a foundational overview of reflective thought theory, cultivates understanding of reflection in practice, then closes the loop by helping the reader to conceptualize the ideas presented and offering applicable takeaways for both students and practitioners. Chapters utilize real-world case studies which detail work environment interactions, planning, and outcomes. These provide opportunities to examine and dissect individual and group dynamics using a reflective practice lens.

*The Reflective Administrat*or offers a fresh perspective on the utility of reflective thought in public service for professional growth and leadership development, and it will be a key resource for students as well as public administration practitioners.

Angela Pool-Funai serves as the Assistant Provost for Academic Programs and Dean of the Graduate School and Office of Scholarship and Sponsored Projects at Fort Hays State University (FHSU) in northwest Kansas. Her academic appointment is in the Department of Sociology at FHSU. Among other publications, she is the author of *Ethics in Fiscal Administration: An Introduction* (2018, Routledge). Dr. P-F holds degrees from Valdosta State University,

Baylor University, and Stephen F. Austin State University. In her spare time, she enjoys canoeing and tinkering on cars.

Tony E. Summers, retired, served as the Chief Executive Officer of the University of the District of Columbia Community College. He previously served as the Vice President for Student Development at the Dallas College, Richland Campus. He completed doctoral studies in Adult Learning and Higher Education at Walden University. An experienced lecturer, educator, facilitator, writer, and consultant, Dr. Summers is also active in numerous community organizations and serves as a board member for several national and local organizations, including the National Council on Student Development, The National Campaign to Prevent Teen and Unplanned Pregnancy, and the Parkland Hospital Community Health Advisory Board. In addition, he was selected to receive a fellowship from the W.K. Kellogg Community College Leadership program.

THE REFLECTIVE ADMINISTRATOR

A Leader-Centered Focus

Angela Pool-Funai and Tony E. Summers

NEW YORK AND LONDON

Designed cover image: © Jackie Niam/Getty Images

First published 2023
by Routledge
605 Third Avenue, New York, NY 10158

and by Routledge
4 Park Square, Milton Park, Abingdon, Oxon, OX14 4RN

Routledge is an imprint of the Taylor & Francis Group, an informa business

© 2023 Angela Pool-Funai and Tony E. Summers

The right of Angela Pool-Funai and Tony E. Summers to be identified as authors of this work has been asserted in accordance with sections 77 and 78 of the Copyright, Designs and Patents Act 1988.

All rights reserved. No part of this book may be reprinted or reproduced or utilised in any form or by any electronic, mechanical, or other means, now known or hereafter invented, including photocopying and recording, or in any information storage or retrieval system, without permission in writing from the publishers.

Trademark notice: Product or corporate names may be trademarks or registered trademarks, and are used only for identification and explanation without intent to infringe.

ISBN: 978-1-032-21983-7 (hbk)
ISBN: 978-1-032-21495-5 (pbk)
ISBN: 978-1-003-27077-5 (ebk)

DOI: 10.4324/9781003270775

Typeset in Bembo
by KnowledgeWorks Global Ltd.

For our families, with appreciation for their unflagging support; and, for the next generation of public service leaders: May you be world-changers.

CONTENTS

List of Figures   *xi*
Acknowledgments   *xii*

Introduction   1

PART I
Theory and Practice of Reflection   **7**

  1 Reflection as Theory   9

  2 Reflection as a Public Service Value   21

  3 Reflection as Good Practice   34

PART II
Tools for Reflection   **47**

  4 Reflection as Hindsight   49

  5 Reflection as Mindfulness   60

  6 Reflection as Perspective   73

PART III
Pathways of Reflection — 87

7	Reflection as Doubt	89
8	Reflection as Self-Analysis	101
9	Reflection as Preparation	112
10	Reflection as Second Wind	125

PART IV
Reflection for Organizational Change — 137

11	Reflection as Culture	139
12	Reflection as Assessment	151
13	Reflection as Forethought	163

Index — *171*

FIGURES

0.1	Bloom's taxonomy	2
1.1	Analysis (critical thinking skills)	17
1.2	Synthesis (critical thinking skills)	17
2.1	Competency, efficiency, and objectivity	25
3.1	Three types of reflective practice	36
4.1	Balancing theory and practice	54
5.1	Action research process	69
6.1	Action learning funnel	79
7.1	A resilient organization is one that learns, develops, and grows together	94
8.1	Using the strengths perspective	103
9.1	Bridging learning and practice	118
10.1	More than three-fourth of public school teachers considered quitting in the 2021–2022 academic year	127
11.1	Creating a culture of reflection	144
12.1	The *I CARE [to act ethically]* model	159
13.1	The reflective practice assessment model	165

ACKNOWLEDGMENTS

We appreciate the hard work and dedication of our copyediting assistant, Nico Pietrantonio, as well as the graphic design creativity of Darlene Gist.

We also owe a debt of gratitude to several individuals for sharing their professional insights as this manuscript developed: Zena Brooks, Tim Davis, Jerry Johnson, Martha Kelly, Wright Lassiter, Marvin Prentice, Brandi Puryear, Dan Stites, and Kalen Summers.

INTRODUCTION

This book is intended to offer a fresh perspective on the concept of reflective thought by taking the practice beyond the classroom and into the actual work of the public sector. The book incorporates reflective practice as a professional development tool within public service careers by walking the reader through an understanding of theories related to reflective thought and the usefulness of reflection in practice, as well as offering practical ways to implement reflection within both the public sector classroom and workplace.

While much of the early study of public administration hinged on its bureaucratic structure, generations of philosophers, theorists, educators, and practitioners have since explored the broader societal influence of the public sphere and the people who work in it. Historical texts such as John Dewey's *How We Think* (2020, originally published in 1910) and Donald Schön's *The Reflective Practitioner* (1984) served as foundational resources on the general topic of reflective thought. There are a myriad of materials on the market instructing educators in using reflection as a teaching tool within an experiential learning or classroom setting. However, the current literature surrounding reflection as a professional practice is lacking a text specifically geared toward the broad field of public service. This book aims to fill that gap.

The book is divided into four parts, each climbing higher on Bloom's Taxonomy hierarchical learning pyramid. Throughout the text, we will transition from foundational theory to a better understanding of self and the organization/system, with an overarching focus on application within fields of public service (Figure 0.1).

DOI: 10.4324/9781003270775-1

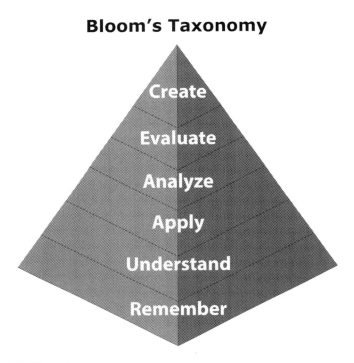

FIGURE 0.1 Bloom's taxonomy

Source: Armstrong, 2010

Part I: Theory and Practice of Reflection

The first three chapters address the *remember* and *understand* layers of Bloom's Taxonomy learning scale. Here, we will examine the theoretical bases of experiential education and reflective practice.

Chapter 1: Reflection as Theory

This introductory chapter will highlight the theoretical underpinnings of reflective thought. The purpose is to help both students and practitioners within public service professions to explore the historical perspectives that evolved into our modern-day public sector, gain an understanding of theories regarding experiential education and other models of learning techniques, recognize reflective practice as a learning tool, and begin spotting opportunities to engage in reflective thought.

Chapter 2: Reflection as a Public Service Value

This chapter will set the stage for the book's angle on the public sector by exploring public service values and how reflection as a professional practice reinforces these principles. Using the Open Government Directive as an example, the chapter will cover key concepts including accountability, transparency, and participation. An exploration of professional skills like competence, efficiency, and objectivity will guide the reader to recognize the importance of upholding the public trust through demonstrating respect, equity, and fairness.

Chapter 3: Reflection as Good Practice

This chapter will introduce the types of reflective practice, to include reflection-on-action, reflection-in-action, and reflection-for-action. The discussion will center on public service values – including professional codes of ethics and related principles – and their relationship to critical reflective and application to the workplace.

Part II: Tools for Reflection

In the second part, we dive deeper into the *application* level and begin to explore what implementing reflective thought within the public sector workforce might look like in practice.

Chapter 4: Reflection as Hindsight

The practice of reflection can be mistaken as simply mulling over one's day; there is a tendency to oversimplify the effort. This chapter will explore the notion of reflection as not merely a recap, but a tool to learn and adapt from past experiences. The text discusses reflection as a transformative tool and invites the reader to explore the emotional complexities of reflective practice, as we begin to put the concepts into action.

Chapter 5: Reflection as Mindfulness

This chapter will revisit some of the theories introduced in Chapter 1 and take the reader from the concept of a cycle in which reflection is a step toward a spiral or ongoing process. Reflective practice is not a standalone concept; on the contrary, it contributes to organizational culture. Adopting a mindfulness aptitude can help to develop an awareness of, and appreciation for, creativity within the public sector workplace. This, in turn, opens opportunities for reflective practice through action research and other means.

Chapter 6: Reflection as Perspective

Incorporating reflection into professional practice means being willing to buck the status quo and accept a transformation of perspective. This chapter will consider changes in mindset as an outcome of reflective practice. Managerial status does not automatically equate to leadership, as the reader learns about leading through change, incorporating action leadership principles, and avoiding destructive leadership tendencies.

Part III: Pathways of Reflection

Chapters 7–10 will take us to the *analyze* stage, where we begin to draw connections between theory and practice. This part will encourage us to question complacency and challenge us to test educational concepts in the real world as we become more reflective administrators.

Chapter 7: Reflection as Doubt

Building on the foundation laid in Chapter 6 about Reflection as Perspective, this chapter will explore theories from Dewey and others in terms of entering a state of doubt during the reflection process. The reader will consider reflective practice as it relates to one's moral code and worldview of what is right, as compared to what is widely accepted.

Chapter 8: Reflection as Self-Analysis

This chapter will discuss the need to enable criticism, both internally and externally, to allow reflective practice to accomplish its full work. It would be futile to regard reflection as simply a pat on the back with no room for learning from error or aiming to grow professionally. This chapter will look at professional growth from a strengths perspective with reflective practice at the core.

Chapter 9: Reflection as Preparation

As noted in Chapter 1, reflection in education gained traction through experiential learning courses. This chapter will focus on training the next generation of public leaders by recommending best practices for implementation in the university classroom. By looking specifically at experiential learning courses as a basis for the discussion, this chapter explores how faculty members might implement reflective practice within an educational setting.

Chapter 10: Reflection as Second Wind

Just as previous chapters considered reflection as a professional development tool for improvement, this chapter will explore reflection as a means to avoid burnout. The public sector is under frequent fire from multiple sides, and recent studies indicate low morale among government workers. By incorporating reflection as a regular practice by public administrators, we hope to instill a renewed sense of job satisfaction among practitioners.

Part IV: Reflection for Organizational Change

Lastly, we will transition to the top of the Bloom's Taxonomy pyramid as we *evaluate* organizational culture within the public sector and *create* a new framework for ourselves to implement in our own professional careers.

Chapter 11: Reflection as Culture

This chapter encourages the understanding, knowledge, and development of inclusive examination to build and sustain a reflective culture. Providing leadership with tools alone does not increase the agility and skill necessary to enhance existential opportunities to build reflective culture. This chapter engages reflection on the topic of leadership's ability and skill sets that create, build, and sustain future-oriented reflective cultures.

Chapter 12: Reflection as Assessment

This chapter will explore the first of two iterations of reflective practice assessment developed by the authors, using the Design-Based Implementation Research (DBIR) approach as a vantage point. These self-assessment tools were designed with both singular learners and collaborative teams in mind, and although the initial design was piloted in an educational setting, this and the following chapter will offer an alternative assessment specifically envisioned for practitioners to implement in the workplace.

Chapter 13: Reflection as Forethought

Ongoing improvement is a hallmark of Design-Based Implementation Research (DBIR), and this chapter will show how the pilot design introduced in the previous chapter evolved into the current model. The new Reflective Practice Assessment model blends ethical reasoning, critical thinking, and continuous quality improvement, within both an individual and team experiential learning process. This chapter will conclude with recommendations for the next steps for the reader to consider as they begin to incorporate reflection into professional practice.

Each chapter will conclude with an applicable case study for further reflection and discussion. These case studies will present actual examples of work environment interactions, planning, and outcomes. These real-world scenarios will provide opportunities to examine and dissect individual and group dynamics using a reflective practice lens. The focus is designed to create, review, and transform ideas, behaviors, and attitudes by presenting fundamental and foundational challenges through each case study that result in the development and understanding of leadership agility skills enhanced by developing oneself and others.

References

Armstrong, P. (2010). Bloom's taxonomy. Vanderbilt University Center for Teaching. Retrieved from https://cft.vanderbilt.edu/guides-sub-pages/blooms-taxonomy/. Shared under a Creative Commons Attribution license.

Dewey, J. (2020). *How we think*. New York: Bibliotech Press.

Schön, D. (1984). *The reflective practitioner: How professionals think in action*. New York: Basic Books.

PART I
Theory and Practice of Reflection

1
REFLECTION AS THEORY

Historical Context on Reflection as a Practice in the Public Sector

When Alexander Hamilton helped set the stage for public administration structure in the context of a new government, he and his Publius co-authors recognized the prevailing distrust of government leaders and the inherent structural imbalances when power is held in too few hands. Throughout his contributions to the *Federalist* papers and as Secretary of the Treasury under George Washington, Hamilton understood the structure of the administration in terms of managing people, processes, and resources.

Since Hamilton's era, however, civil service has evolved into a profession in its own right. Woodrow Wilson, who served as the 28th President of the United States from 1913 to 1921, is widely credited as the patriarch of public administration – though not universally so, as Hamilton scholars would object. (After all, Hamilton was largely responsible for crafting the federal financial framework of the young United States and served as its first Treasury Secretary.) Wilson believed strongly that politics and public administration should be separate, yet cooperative, endeavors. This split between the elected and the employed is often referred to as the politics-administration dichotomy, and it is the foundation for what is generically known as the bureaucracy.

A contemporary of Wilson, Max Weber took the separation of politics and administration a step further. He imagined the ideal bureaucracy as a strictly hierarchical and rational structure and worried about the potential for overreach in influence by public administrators. Sager and Rosser (2009) described Weber's belief that "... in order to make the state work efficiently and rationally and to control the public servant's influence, a strict separation of the political

DOI: 10.4324/9781003270775-3

and the administrative spheres seemed indispensable." Weber's perspective considered public administration through an objective and quantifiable lens. For example, one way an organization's efficiency can be measured is by its output: How many clients were served in the current year, compared to years prior? How long was the average wait time? How much external funding did the Advancement office raise last quarter versus the same time frame two years ago?

However, this black-and-white view fails to take into consideration the subjective nuances and qualitative benefits of public service. Consider these examples, in contrast: How do local homeowners describe their quality of life before and after the development of a new neighborhood park? Ask Chamber of Commerce members in a college town to define their town-and-gown relationship with the university – what benefits do they provide each other? As we will begin to unpack later in this chapter and throughout the text, reflective practice tools can take us from merely objective goals to check off like a to-do list, toward a subjective willingness to learn, grow, and continuously improve.

Wilson was a forerunner of the Progressive reform movement and believed that public administration should operate in a highly efficient, systematic, scientific manner. In his 1887 essay, he used the imagery of the human body to explain how administrative functions share likeness, though function separately (Wilson, 1887). For example, the pulmonary and circulatory systems have unique processes, yet they are intricately coordinated and contribute to the overall health of each other and the body, as a whole. McCandless and Guy (2013) describe Wilson's perspective this way:

> Wilson never intended to erect a firewall between administration and politics. Rather, he distinguished the province and process of one so as to study it in isolation from the other. Administration, as Wilson characterized it, included neutral competence, discretion of administrators unaffected by partisan politics, and a differentiation of duties between administrators and their political masters marked by significant co-dependence and interconnectedness of duties and concerns.
>
> *p. 370*

So, while Wilson advocated for a clear demarcation between the roles of politicians and bureaucrats, he also acknowledged a measure of necessary overlap, particularly in terms of public administrators' involvement in the policymaking process. This perspective has carried forward several generations after Wilson. In the modern American administrative state, unelected staff members are a linchpin in federal, state, and local governments. As a frame of reference, the Congressional Research Service (2021) reported that in the House of Representatives alone, more than 9,000 such public administrators work across committees, Member offices, and other venues. Congressional staffers on the Senate side currently total more than 5,700, according to the Congressional

Research Service (2020). While it may sound like a lot of employees, those nearly 15,000 federal-level positions do not hold a candle to the additional number of public service professionals at the state level, much less than 3,000 counties across the US or nearly 20,000 municipalities.

A purely mechanical, formalized approach to bureaucratic operations such as the version Weber idealized leaves little room for reflective practice. However, the modern field of public administration has undergone a necessary shift in mindset. McCandless and Guy (2013) describe it as "… becoming more attentive to its role as the convener and facilitator of collaborative, deliberative processes designed to enable citizens to self-govern." This perspective is much more conducive to reflective practice, as they go on to explain, "This highlights the relationship between administrators and citizens, and targets the relationship between government and society as opposed to the relationships inside government" (p. 372).

> **MIRROR MOMENT**
>
> The politics-administration dichotomy has been interpreted numerous ways by scholars over the years. Some say that the roles of elected officials and public administrators should be completely disengaged from one another. Others suggest that the separation has more to do with influence over decisions or power dynamics, with an emphasis on checks and balances between entities. How do you interpret the divide, and what do you think is the ideal framework to fulfill the work of the public sector?

Theoretical Underpinnings of Reflective Thought

Experience alone does not equate learning. As Ash and Clayton (2009) elaborate, "Learning – and understanding learning processes – does not happen maximally through experience alone but rather as a result of thinking about – reflecting on – it" (p. 27). Reflective practice has its foundation in constructivist theory. The constructivist view of learning is compatible with the notion of self-direction; it emphasizes the combined characteristics of active inquiry, independence, and individuality in a learning task. Reflective practice is a cognitive process examining perspectives of meaning. From a constructivist perspective, a central part of the learning process is creating thoughtful and authentic change using personal reflection, as well as through dialogue and encouragement from others. The primary concepts of reflection-in-action, reflection-on-action, and reflection-for-action are to see life experience as both a resource and a stimulus for learning: the individuality of constructivism coupled with the learner's interaction through shared experiences (Merriam,

Caffarella, & Baumgartner, 2007). We will unpack each of these terms shortly, and these three forms of reflective practice will serve as the foundation for our discussion from here on out.

Experiential Learning Theory

It is apparent that individuals learn from experience, though scholars differ on the details of exactly *how* people learn contingent on their theoretical position. To support a stance on learning as a product of experience, Dewey (1938) argued that the experience must demonstrate a degree of timelessness, as it is an ongoing effort of change and growth: "The principle of the continuity of experience means that every experience both takes up something from those which have gone before and modifies in some way the quality of those which some after" (p. 13). In the dimension of reflective practice, learning is ever-reaching. It does not exist in a vacuum and is not isolated within individual approaches or isolated moments in time. Each element, reflection-in-action, reflection-on-action, and reflection-for-action, provides learners with active, real-time experience.

The three types of reflective practice mentioned above serve as a foundational building block to engage learner progression from what they have learned in the context of current experience to connect with those in the past, as well as anticipating future implications. For example, we can make the assumption that individuals with postsecondary education degrees are able to connect their previous academic experiences with those of their current engagement; consequently, they will also be able to apply what they are currently experiencing to future learning opportunities. Understanding this interaction between past, present, and future offers a perspective on professional growth for individuals, as well as a trajectory of continuous improvement within our organizations. We are not static as individuals, and we live and work within dynamic environments. We must change in order to grow on a personal level, and our institutions and organizations must be willing to adapt in order to remain relevant to the communities they serve.

Dewey (1938) recognized this need for learning to evolve in order to accommodate new circumstances: "An experience is always what it is because of a transaction taking place between an individual and what, at the time, constitutes his environment ..." (p. 27). The learning experience can look different for multiple individuals in the same environment – consider students in a classroom or even siblings in the same household. Likewise, a single individual can be exposed to a variety of learning experiences by being present in different settings, such as on-the-job training in an office, participating in a virtual webinar conference, or taking a field trip to a nature reserve. This relationship between learning spaces and learning styles brings us to the work of Kolb and Kolb (2005), arguably the premiere scholars in reflective practice through experiential learning in an educational setting.

Often depicted in a circle with four sections, what has become popularly known as Kolb's learning cycle features reflection as but one of four stages in a loop of new experiences. The Kolb cycle includes steps of concrete experience, reflective observation, abstract conceptualization, and active experimentation. In a study on experiential learning spaces within higher education settings, Kolb and Kolb (2005) envisioned the four phases as sides of a square divided into nine blocks, with varying degrees of overlap between students' feeling, acting, reflecting, and thinking within the grid. Even in this more integrated variation of the Kolb cycle, however, reflective practice is not woven throughout the entire learning process. (As we will explore further in Chapters 12 and 13, the authors envision reflective practice as an integral component of each layer of learning. Reflection is embedded within our comprehensive individual and collective learning processes, rather than a standalone phase.)

Scaffolding on the work of other scholars, Kolb also projected that learning from experience necessitated four distinct abilities or traits to dovetail with the four phases of the learning cycle. Merriam et al. (2007) interpret these as:

1. openness and willingness to involve oneself in new experiences (concrete experience);
2. observational and reflective skills so these new experiences can be viewed from a variety of perspectives (reflective observation);
3. analytical abilities so integrative ideas and concepts can be created from their observations (abstract conceptualization); and
4. decision-making and problem-solving skills so these new ideas and concepts can be used in actual practice (active experimentation).

As with reflective action, the final phase or step can become an additional set of definitive experiences that can, in turn, begin the experiential cycle of learning again.

Turesky and Gallagher (2011) infused Kolb's experiential learning theory into their work on leadership coaching by explaining that the Kolb cycle provides a particularly useful framework for developing the skills necessary for leaders to navigate complex situations and administrative relationships in an effective manner. Experiential learning theory as a tool within reflective practice begins to unfold from a recognition of uniqueness, complexity, and variability of specific learning and administrative situations.

Transformative Learning

Transformative learning encompasses adjustment through change, which results in an impactful, foundational redirection in our personal visions of ourselves, as well as our perceptions of the environments we live, work, study, and play within. This concept stands in direct contrast to informational learning, which Kegan (2000) refers to as "extending already established cognitive capacities into terrain" (p. 48). Transformative learning calls attention to amendment or remodeling of our understanding and existence of knowledge. As Merriam et al. (2007) explain, the mental building of an experience, inner meaning, and reflection are common components of transformational learning.

According to Mezirow (2000), transformative learning can occur when one of two shifts in mindset take place: the learner experiences an adjustment to their attitudes or beliefs, or they develop a fresh perspective. Mezirow elaborates on this change in one's mental vantage point: "A frame of reference is composed of two dimensions, a habit of mind and resulting points of view. A *habit of mind* is a set of assumptions–broad, generalized, orienting predispositions that act as a filter for interpreting the meaning of experience."

Prior to employing reflective action stages (in-action, on-action, and for-action), the learner engages in a process of taking for granted frames of reference – these include existing habits, mindsets, and actions. The goal is to engage transformative learning as a foundational theory to support reflective practice, to unlock our values, goals, and processes. It is also designed to generate beliefs and opinions that are proven to be authentic, true, inclusive, open, and wholly capable of change, with justification to guide individual and group actions to carry on our work.

There are four main elements within transformative learning theory: experience, critical reflection, reflective discourse, and action. As we touched on earlier and will explore in more detail in later chapters, this quartet of components also closely parallels experiential learning theory. Learners must critically reflect on their experience and talk with others about their worldview in order to gain the best judgment possible, before acting on new perspectives.

> **MIRROR MOMENT**
>
> Earlier in this chapter, we discussed letting go of preexisting conditions, in terms of our worldview. If we are to move from informational learning to transformative learning, then we need to understand that it might mean the difference between repainting a wall in our minds versus taking a sledgehammer to the drywall and tearing it down. This might come across as a harsh approach, understandably. What walls have you built up in your own worldview that you would have difficulty remodeling?

Andragogy

Reflective practice permits learners to make decisions in complex and everyday situations. Often the decisions or judgements are grounded in experience and knowledge. This concept frames the definition of Adult Education, which is built around a curriculum that engages students' needs and interests. Adults find themselves in specific experiences with respect to work, family, social engagements, community life, and other environments, each requiring adjustments to sustain meaningful and mindful learning relationships. If education contributes to one's quality of life, then we can surmise that life, in and of itself, is also education. Andragogy focuses on the adult learner and their life situation (Merriam et al., 2007).

Merriam (2001) laid out five assumptions outlining that andragogy describes adult learners as someone who:

1. has an independent self-concept and who can direct their own learning;
2. has accumulated a reservoir of life experiences that is a rich resource for learning;
3. has learning needs closely related to changing social roles;
4. is problem-centered and interested in immediate application of knowledge; and
5. is motivated to learn by internal rather than external factors (p. 89).

From these assumptions, Knowles, Holton III, and Swanson (2005) proposed a program planning model for designing, implementing, and evaluating educational experiences with adults. Reflective practice embraces their assumptions for design, implications, and evaluation of learning activities. The climate for reflective practice mirrors adulthood, throughout both its physical and psychological presentation. At the core of andragogy lies a belief that adults should feel accepted, appreciated, supported, and respected. These assumptions provided educators with a sense of identity and in doing so, distinguished andragogy from other areas of education.

Reflective practice makes special allowance for individual contributions from learners and seeks to organize these contributions into some form of social purpose within the framework of andragogy. Andragogy became a rallying point for those educators and training development specialists trying to define the field of adult education as separate from other focal points of education. Although reflective practice is certainly not limited to adults, the theoretical foundation of andragogy as a model for curriculum design has made important contributions to the evolution of reflection in the field of education, particularly with regard to experiential learning.

Encouraging Active Learning through Personal Relationships

Communication is an important ingredient within reflective practice, particularly in terms of navigating interpersonal relationships. Brookfield (1987) once noted that a basis of communication between partners (in any type of relationship) is a prerequisite for understanding one another's perspectives and being able to navigate changes that arise in the relationship. Without effective communication as a foundation in the relationship, reconciling differences of opinion and attempting to negotiate challenges become exercises in futility. This observation may be most apparent in a familial relationship, but the same concepts hold true in the workplace or school environment. If an employee feels like their comments go in one ear and out the other when talking to a supervisor, then they may become reticent to raise concerns or make recommendations, and the agency potentially misses out on important feedback that could help improve its performance.

Put another way, relationships are like rigorous essays, identified by continuous revisions, adjustments in focal points, and intervals of reframing and renegotiating. The concept of critical analysis is demanded within reflective practice and is also an important tool to help strengthen lines of communication. The assumptions we make within our own frame of mind configure our behaviors, and the same goes for our colleagues. Navigating these differences of perspective are important as we seek to strengthen the relationship between reflective practice and critical thinking. The purpose of reflective practice is not in needing to be right or in winning, but in using critical thinking skills and maintaining an openness to a variety of perspectives (Figures 1.1 and 1.2).

> **MIRROR MOMENT**
>
> We have read that reflective practice is not about bragging rights; instead, it centers on using critical thinking skills and being willing to consider new perspectives. Think about your current educational institution, workplace, or organization: Where are there vocal differences of opinions, silos of operations, or factions among employees? Taking what you have learned thus far, how might you begin using reflective practice and critical thinking to help break down some of those barriers?

Reflective practice and critical thinking can occur within scenarios that are important in a variety of real-world contexts: our work, relationships, politics, and the media (Brookfield, 1987). Learners never reach a point of final development. Continued use of both well established and new theories aid our thinking and growth of reflective practice. Merriam et al. (2007) remind us that reflective practice requires a deliberate slowing down to consider multiple perspectives and active, conscious processing of thoughts including: analysis, synthesis, and metacognition. Analysis means to take a large concept and break it down into smaller parts, whereas synthesis involves taking separate

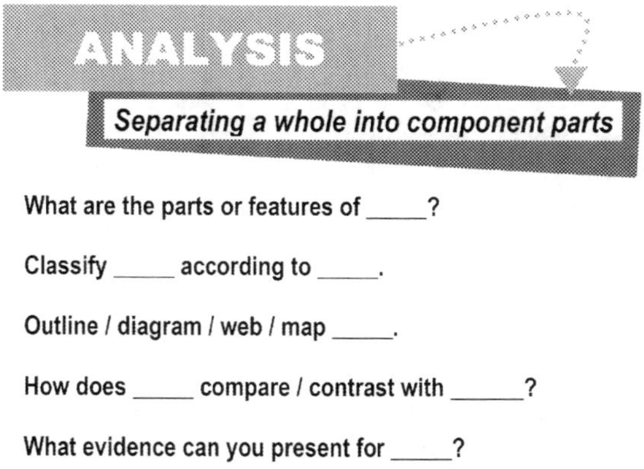

ANALYSIS

Separating a whole into component parts

What are the parts or features of _____?

Classify _____ according to _____.

Outline / diagram / web / map _____.

How does _____ compare / contrast with _____?

What evidence can you present for _____?

FIGURE 1.1 Analysis (critical thinking skills)

SYNTHESIS

Combining ideas to form a new whole

What would you predict / infer from _____?

What ideas can you add to _____?

How would you create / design a new _____?

What might happen if you combined _____ with _____?

What solutions would you suggest for _____?

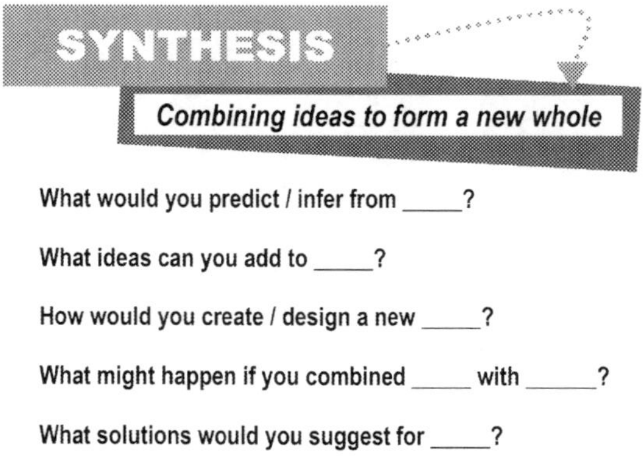

FIGURE 1.2 Synthesis (critical thinking skills)

ideas and creating something new. Metacognition is often defined as thinking about thinking or having an awareness of what you do (and don't!) know. Fogarty and Pete (2020) explain: "The act of thinking about what you do and think about your own thinking and learning is the mark of a mindful, reflective, and considered decision maker" (p. xi).

Learning Partnership Model

Based on the findings of a longitudinal study of young adults and ideas first outlined in her book, Baxter Magolda (2004) introduced the Learning Partnership Model. Her concept developed from a concern of fostering the development of self-authorship and established that environments supporting this individualized perspective would then challenge dependence on authority

(Patton, Renn, Guido, & Quaye, 2016). Three primary assumptions guided this approach:

- Knowledge is multi-layered and erected within social environments.
- The individual is crucial for knowledge creation.
- Justification and competence are apportioned in the shared creation of knowledge among peers (Patton et al., 2016, p. 375).

These concepts address key components of reflective practice – each addresses cognitive, interpersonal, and intrapersonal stages presented in interactions associated with reflection-in action, reflection-on-action, and reflection-for-action. Each stage of reflective practice is built upon constructing connections, sharing experiences, examining expertise, defining authority, and identifying knowledge. Baxter Magolda (2004) noted that each concept challenges how individuals determine meaning for themselves, and this effort is a developmental process that builds self-authorship.

Case Study

Martin is a recent college graduate and has acquired an entry-level position with a large industrial equipment manufacturer. He entered the workforce directly from a traditional institutional educational environment, but his classroom settings were not innovative, creative, or highly structured. The environments were often loosely organized with lectures and recitation assignments. Within his first year of employment, Martin was confronted with taking personal responsibility for organizational beliefs, values, and actions. He was expected to adopt and adhere to the mission and conform to the company's organizational structure.

While he possessed strong technical skills, there existed a gap for Martin within the new organizational environment. His postsecondary educational institution provided theoretical frameworks and practical skills (based on academic major), yet it did not provide the required knowledge and skills necessary to align Martin with the transformative learning techniques and applied knowledge that organizations require in today's work environment. Martin needed the skills necessary to form a new frame of mind required so that he could take initiative, direct his work, evaluate other people's perspectives, and self-direct.

Based on what you have learned thus far in this chapter:

1. What might be required to form learning partnerships between postsecondary institutions and hiring organizations to help prepare graduates like Martin?

2. How can academic departments and support services develop learning partnerships to enhance curriculum, classroom engagement, and services that recognize the importance of adult growth for the work environment for people like Martin?
3. What role can transformative learning play in the development of learning partnerships?

Conclusion

Understanding the theoretical underpinnings of reflective thought helps us to better understand how these concepts unfold in the real world. The intentional practice of reflection is also useful as a means to develop one's own ethical framework, and the following chapters aim to broaden perspectives about what reflective practice entails while offering the reader practical tools to implement in a professional environment. In Chapter 2, we will consider public service values and explore how reflection as a professional practice reinforces these principles.

References

Ash, S. L., & Clayton, P. H. (2009). Generating, deepening, and documenting learning: The power of critical reflection in applied learning. *Journal of Applied Learning in Higher Education*, 1, 25–48, 27.

Baxter Magolda, M. B. (2004). Learning partnerships model: A framework for promoting self-authorship. In M. Baxter Magolda & P. M. King (Eds.), *Learning partnerships: Theory and models of practice to educate for self-authorship* (pp. 37–62). Sterling, VA: Stylus.

Brookfield, D. S. (1987). *Developing critical thinkers: Challenging adults to explore alternative ways of thinking and acting.* San Francisco, CA: Jossey-Bass.

Congressional Research Service. (2020, October 19). *Senate staff levels in member, committee, leadership, and other offices, 1977–2020.* Retrieved from https://sgp.fas.org/crs/misc/R43946.pdf

Congressional Research Service. (2021, September 2). *House of representatives staff levels in member, committee, leadership, and other offices, 1977–2021.* Retrieved from https://crsreports.congress.gov/product/pdf/R/R43947

Dewey, J. (1938). *Experience and education.* New York: Collier Books.

Fogarty, R. J., & Pete, B. M. (2020). *Metacognition: The neglected skill set for empowering students, revised edition (your planning guide to teaching mindful, reflective, proficient thinkers and problem solvers). ProQuest Ebook Central.* Bloomington: Solution Tree Press. p. xi. Retrieved from https://ebookcentral.proquest.com/lib/fhsu/detail.action?docID=6215730

Kegan, R. (2000). What "form" transforms? A constructive-developmental approach to transformational learning. In J. Mezirow (Ed.), *Learning as transformation: Critical perspectives on a theory in progress* (pp. 35–70, 48). San Francisco, CA: Jossey-Bass.

Knowles, M., Holton, E., III, & Swanson, R. (2005). *The adult learner.* Burlington, Canada: Taylor & Francis Group.

Kolb, A. Y., & Kolb, D. A. (June 2005). Learning styles and learning spaces: Enhancing experiential learning in higher education. *Academy of Management Learning & Education, 4*(2), 193–212. Retrieved from http://www.jstor.org/stable/40214287

McCandless, S. A., & Guy, M. E. (2013). One more time: What did Woodrow Wilson really mean about politics and administration? *Administrative Theory & Praxis, 35*(3), 356–377.

Merriam, B. S. (2001). Andragogy and self-directed learning: Pillars of adult learning theory. *New Directions for Adult and Continuing Education, 2001*(89), 3–14. Jossey-Bass.

Merriam, B. S., Caffarella, S. R., & Baumgartner, M. L. (2007). *Learning in adulthood: A comprehensive guide.* San Francisco, CA: Wiley & Sons.

Mezirow, J. (2000). *Learning as transformation: Critical perspectives on a theory in progress.* San Francisco, CA: Jossey-Bass.

Patton, D. L., Renn, A. R., Guido, M., & Quaye, F. (2016). *Student development in college: Theory, research, and practice.* San Francisco, CA: Wiley & Sons.

Sager, F., & Rosser, C. (2009). Weber, Wilson, and Hegel: Theories of modern bureaucracy. *Public Administration Review, 69*(6), 1136–1147, 1139.

Turesky, F., & Gallagher, T. (2011). Know thyself: Coaching for leadership using Kolb's cognitive learning theory. *The Coaching Psychologist, 7*(1), 5–14.

Wilson, W. (1887). The study of administration. *Political Science Quarterly, 2*(2), 197–222.

2
REFLECTION AS A PUBLIC SERVICE VALUE

Public service values dovetail naturally with reflection as a professional practice. In fact, NASPAA (Network of Schools of Public Policy, Affairs, and Administration) accreditation standards mandate that public administration graduate students are expected to be able to "reflect upon the social and ethical responsibilities and the equity implications linked to the application of their knowledge and judgments" (NASPAA, Standard 5, n.d.-a). This expectation of reflection as an integral part of professional development will be explored throughout this chapter. NASPAA further describes public service values as "pursuing the public interest with accountability and transparency; serving professionally with competence, efficiency, and objectivity; acting ethically so as to uphold the public trust; and demonstrating respect, equity, and fairness in dealings with citizens and fellow public servants" (NASPAA, Preconditions, n.d.-b). We will take each of these values in turn later in this chapter, but first we will explore how public service values mesh with reflection as a professional practice.

In the previous chapter, we introduced the concept of reflection as an ongoing endeavor, rather than a single step along the learning curve. The same principle holds true when we consider reflection as a professional practice beyond the classroom setting. A reflective administrator will recognize that public service values are not checkboxes that you can mark complete and then forget about. Public service leaders are expected to regard the public interest by upholding traits like accountability and transparency, as noted above. Earning a reputation as someone who adheres to accountability is not a singular effort; likewise, behaving in a transparent manner requires consistent awareness of situations where closed lines of communication pose a risk.

DOI: 10.4324/9781003270775-4

In a similar vein, developing skills to become more competent, efficient, and objective requires a willingness to adapt and be open to change. An employee would not be praised for only *occasionally* demonstrating competence while generally wasting time, giving a half-hearted effort, and showing favoritism to certain clients over others. Other public service values such as behaving ethically and showing respect, equity, and fairness throughout each interaction with the public will involve active, reflective practice. None of these public service values operate in isolation, nor are they temporary in nature. Reflection emphasizes the need for employees to explore interpretive judgements about complex business, management, and personal issues.

As NASPAA notes, "we measure inclusion not just by who is present, but by whether they are participating" (NASPAA, Revised Accreditation Standards, n.d.-c). Policy & Procedure manuals and lip service at staff meetings matter little if organizations neglect to engage relevant stakeholders in the hands-on mission work of the agency. Accreditation standards are a clear example of this expectation, as the external review process typically requires artifacts or other demonstrative evidence that the organization is not only fulfilling the requirements of its competencies but also actively including stakeholders throughout all phases of the decision-making process.

It isn't enough to say that we agree with public service values like transparency, accountability, participation, and equity – or even to incorporate the terms into our mission statements. Public service professionals need to adhere to such values through a dedicated process of critical reflection in practice. Critical reflection encourages individuals to problem solve, analyze, arrive at decisions, and overcome obstacles. One can acquire, interpret, and use information, facts, and data to resolve problems to demonstrate originality and intuitiveness. Reflection as a practice needs to be a comprehensive and inclusive aspect of our professional roles, which we will discuss in greater detail in Chapters 12 and 13. Next, we will break down NASPAA's public service values and consider how reflection can be incorporated into each principle.

Pursuing Accountability and Transparency

Accountability and transparency are inherent in the concept of investing public trust, and these traits are particularly in the forefront of the public's mind regarding roles such as law enforcement officers. For example, the International Association of Chiefs of Police (IACP) has had a Code of Ethics for law enforcement officers in effect since 1957. In part, it states: "I recognize the badge of my office as a symbol of public faith, and I accept it as a public trust to be held so long as I am true to the ethics of police service" (IACP, n.d.-a, n.d.-b). Public faith and trust only happens when members of the community are privy to the work of the public sector – both the praiseworthy and the areas that need much improvement – and that transfer of knowledge comes through transparency and accountability.

Police Chief Magazine reports that some law enforcement agencies are proactively engaging in "accountability-driven leadership" (Serpas, n.d.) to strike a balance between efficiency and effectiveness within their local communities. In this context, efficiency refers to measurable productivity, such as tracking the number of tickets written or traffic stops made. Effectiveness, on the other hand, refers to outcomes, including goals like lowering the number of traffic deaths related to motorists driving under the influence. Together, improved efficiency and effectiveness contribute toward greater overall accountability for public service agencies.

The IACP Standards of Conduct go on to say that "Law enforcement officers must accept and abide by a high ethical and moral standard that is consistent with the rule of law they are sworn to uphold" (IACP, n.d.). This means that police officers should abide by behaviors that are beyond reproach, lest they find themselves in conflict with the very laws they have sworn to uphold. This implies that on- and off-duty, a law enforcement officer should hold themselves accountable to the same measures by which they gauge the public. Maintaining such a threshold of public accountability involves a great deal of reflection-in-action, on-action, and for-action by individual law enforcement officers and the broader profession through efforts of groups like the IACP.

MIRROR MOMENT

How would you define public trust, as it relates to law enforcement personnel? Consider the role of a law enforcement officer: How might an individual officer positively reinforce public faith and trust? In terms of accountability and transparency, how could a department, precinct, or the overarching profession ameliorate concerns from the public in light of law enforcement officers' alleged overreach of power?

Accountability and transparency are key ingredients in public sector leadership. Both are linked to the definition of reflective leadership. Transparency in the public sector cannot happen unless there is access, because it is not an accidental feature. Accountability should not mean simply a search for someone to blame when things go wrong. It is about empowering people to carry out their task, and is based on a shared understanding of what tasks are and how they are to be carried out with an understanding about why they are important, as well as a mutual understanding about what successful outcomes look like. Transparency and accountability together impact empowerment, and empowered stakeholders are participatory stakeholders. (We will discuss participation and empowerment in more detail in Chapter 10.)

Speaking about the public sector at large, accountability and transparency are included in the Open Government Directive, an initiative spearheaded by former President Obama in 2009 with the intention of making the federal government more transparent, efficient, and accessible. Despite the Open Government Directive being archived by the subsequent Trump administration, the Federal Communications Commission (FCC) remained one federal agency that took to heart its charge to "address both the letter and the spirit of the Directive" (FCC, 2011). Among other tools, the FCC embarked on releasing data sets to the public and making its web presence more accessible, including offering an avenue for public feedback. In so doing, the FCC aimed to increase participation by opening opportunities for everyday individuals to engage with the agency, thereby increasing its level of accountability and transparency among the public.

Cultivating Professional Competence, Efficiency, and Objectivity

For better or for worse, public administration professionals are often judged by the general public based on personal perceptions of whether the individual demonstrated competency, efficiency, and objectivity in the course of their interactions on the job. The Department of Motor Vehicles (DMV), for example, with its stereotypically long lines, extensive paperwork, time-consuming, and often complicated processes, as well as expense, has long been the butt of jokes about bureaucracy's alleged problems. These sweeping accusations of public administrators' incompetence, inefficiencies, and inequitable behavior are not fair across the board, but the negative label persists throughout the public sector (Figure 2.1).

Competence

Professional competency covers a wide swath of skills and traits. Bowman, West, and Beck (2010) refer to being able to fulfill the assigned duties of one's job as *technical* competency. We often hear terms such as "hard skills" (the technical or quantitative aspects of the job) and "soft skills" (the qualitative elements of the role) when it comes to professional training. Job postings include required skills and experience for the position, but they also often include preferred qualities. Hard skills, or technical competency, might include relevant educational credentials, a minimum number of years' experience in a particular industry, demonstrated mastery of proprietary software or a specialized certification. Soft skills, on the other hand, include traits such as interpersonal communication, time management, or ability to resolve conflict.

Cultural competency is another example of a soft skill, which Winters (2020) defines as "… a continuous learning process to gain knowledge, skills,

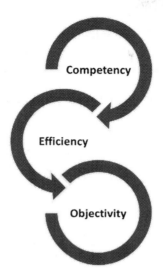

FIGURE 2.1 Competency, efficiency, and objectivity

and understanding to discern cultural difference in one's own and other cultures and to use in problem solving, decision-making, and conflict resolution" (p. 21). Thomas Bernard and Moriah (2007) posit that such competency should address oppression, power, and privilege from a relationship perspective. Through this lens, checking the boxes of a particular job description's skill set isn't enough to make one adequately prepared for a position in public service. A competitive candidate should also approach their position from a reflective vantage point of how others may be affected by their work, decisions, or policies. As we discussed in the last chapter, reflective practice is neither an isolated experience, nor is it conducted in a vacuum. Reflective administrators need to be mindful of how their interactions with others either contribute to or help tear down historic systems of prejudice, inequitable power dynamics, and favoritism.

Adapted from Triolo (2012), culture is the interplay of structure, reward systems, the people themselves, information systems, leadership, and processes by which the organization operates – and, consequently, how we operate within it. We will explore reflection as culture in more depth in Chapter 11, but in the context of the current discussion, let's consider Schein's (2010) description of culture as the way organization members exhibit facets of motivation, trust, and communication in how they interact and accomplish the work of the organization. Culture is a shared learning experience within groups and is established and reinforced by behaviors that others witness as effective or permitted by a department and/or organization. Culture is formulated by how tasks are completed and difficult situations are remediated.

Consider an academic advisor at a public university, for example. This professional likely works with dozens, if not hundreds, of different students – all of whom have their own goals, priorities, and challenges. Academic advising may very well be the higher education version of the DMV, when it comes to dissatisfaction among clientele. In the early-2000s, the University of Wisconsin–Oshkosh recognized that their academic support services desperately needed an overhaul (Freeman, 2008). Advising loads were too heavy; faculty participation was lackluster; and, perhaps most telling, students were feeling frustrated. As part of the comprehensive redesign of UW-Oshkosh's undergraduate advising resource center, the university outlined learning outcomes for academic advisors, which included the following:

- "understanding and applying student development and learning theory;
- using feedback to understand students' needs and to improve their advising practices;
- initiating and maintaining contact with faculty in their advising areas; and
- staying current on curricula" (Freeman, 2008, p. 1)

This re-centered focus on developing a holistic awareness of students' unique situations reiterates the relationship perspective noted above. Freeman went on to note that while academic advising improved markedly over the next five years, the university was aware that it must commit to continuous improvement efforts in the area of student support services. (Earnestly seeking to follow a trajectory of ongoing improvement is a positive indication of reflection-for-action!)

Based on hard skills alone, professional competency could be summed up using quantitative factors such as speed in completing assignments, accuracy in finished tasks, or a comparably measurable benchmark. When soft skills like interpersonal communication and cultural competency are taken into consideration, an effective public administrator must consider the more qualitative aspects of their role, including their interactions with those who have different perspectives than themselves. In the example of UW-Oshkosh, this means engaging offices across university units – from academic affairs to student affairs – and being willing to make adjustments along the way, as feedback is received and curriculum changes.

While cultural competency has a well-established foundation within the healthcare field (Karnick, 2016), it is also important to consider this concept in terms of relating to individuals through other public sector professions, as well. The American Psychological Association (2015) describes cultural competency "… as the ability to understand, appreciate and interact with people from cultures or belief systems different from one's own." Cultural competency consists of informal values, beliefs, and norms that shape how employees provide internal and external service, customer care, and relationship building – and these relationships permeate the communities within which the organization is responsible for building public trust and providing a value-added benefit. The Centers for Disease Control and Prevention (CDC, n.d.) go on to explain: "Cultural and linguistic competence is a set of congruent behaviors, attitudes, and policies that come together in a system, agency, or among professionals that enables effective work in cross-cultural situations." How much more pertinent is it, then, for public sector professionals to attain competence in serving individuals from diverse communities?

> **MIRROR MOMENT**
>
> In your own words, what does it mean to be a competent public administrator? Specifically, what does competency mean not only in terms of one's technical job description but also cultural competency and/or relating to others on an interpersonal level? Consider your own job description (or research a job posting for a position you aspire to): What hard and soft skills are necessary for you to be successful in that role?

Efficiency

As mentioned in the law enforcement example above, efficiency pertains to the manner in which goals are carried out – the measurable steps taken to complete an objective. Yet, if we consider efficiency and effectiveness through a more holistic lens, we might begin to recognize the crossover between the quantitative and qualitative aspects of the public sector. Let's examine the proliferation of the Strengths Perspective within the social work profession as one example of efficiency from a qualitative angle. We will delve into this topic in much more detail in Chapter 8, but it is apropos to introduce here, particularly with regard to improved efficiency. Generally speaking, a Strengths Perspective focuses on inclusivity and positivity, and as Chapin (1995) puts it, this framework "… posits that the strengths and resources of people and their environment rather than their problems and pathologies should be the central focus of the helping process …" (p. 506). In other words, the clients themselves become an active element of the solution, which contributes to efficiency.

According to the School of Social Welfare at the University of Kansas, "[t]he main principles of the Strengths Perspective (in a therapeutic context) are for social workers to:

- Recognize that every individual, group, family, and community has strengths and resources

- Engage in systematic assessment of strengths and resources
- Realize that while trauma, abuse, illness and struggle may be injurious, they may also be sources of challenge and opportunity
- Honor client-set goals and aspirations for growth and change
- Serve clients' and communities' interests through collaboration with them as directors of their own helping process
- Mobilize the strengths and resources of clients, relationships, and environments
- Link goals to specific doable actions that activate strengths and resources
- Engage in social work with a sense of caring and hope" (KU SSW, n.d.)

Regarding the Strengths Perspective, Saleeby (2002) explained: "Focusing and building on client strengths ... is an imperative of the several values that govern our work and the operations of a democratic, just, and pluralistic society including distributive justice, equality, respect for the dignity of the individual, inclusiveness and diversity, and the search for maximum autonomy within maximum community." (264). That said, what might it look like if we expounded upon the Strengths Perspective and applied it to the broader field of public service?

> **MIRROR MOMENTS**
>
> Using the principles listed above, consider how each statement could be revamped to pertain to other public service professions. (For example, how might our communities change if public housing authorities "recognize[d] that every individual, group, family, and community has strengths and resources"? What would it mean for a city manager to "engage in systematic assessment of strengths and resources"?)

Objectivity

We began this section discussing negative stereotypes that society often holds toward public administrators. If we take an honest look at our own biases, however, we may realize that we also have work to do regarding prejudicial leanings of varying types. "Bias is not limited to one domain of life. It is not limited to one profession, one race, or one country," explained scholar and author Eberhardt (2019). "People can hold biases based on all sorts of characteristics—skin color, age, weight, ethnic origin, accent, disability, height, gender." (48)

Those who have devoted their careers to public service are not exempt from bias. Eberhardt put it this way: "Bias, even when we are not conscious of it, has consequences that we need to understand and mitigate. The stereotypic associations we carry in our heads can affect what we perceive, how we think, and the actions we take." (7) Objectivity may also be described as neutrality or impartiality. Eberhardt went on to suggest, "Confronting implicit bias requires us to look in the mirror ... to face how readily stereotypes and unconscious associations can shape our reality." (7)

While bias may certainly manifest through an individual's engagement with the general public, it could also be evident within the public sector organization, at large. One potential trouble spot to note is in the area of human resources, as Pearson (2019) explains: "Hiring an employee is a multilayered process involving the use of objective information and subjective perception" (p. 25). Hiring, training, promotion, and merit processes are all at risk of biased influence. Bias tears down trust and contributes to a toxic work environment, which in turn creates a negative experience for clients, students, volunteers, and anyone else who interacts with the agency or organization. Understanding and recognizing that we all have implicit biases will help us become more reflective administrators who are better able to perform the work of public service through a lens of objectivity, rather than subjectivity and prejudice.

Upholding the Public Trust (Ethically)

A strong ethical foundation is not only representative of public service values, but ethical leadership also dovetails as a natural fit beneath the broader umbrella of human values. As public administrators, we have the opportunity each and every day to allow our interactions with others to mirror our integrity, and doing so consistently helps build public trust.

Michael Lipsky (2010) popularized the notion of street-level bureaucrats in his seminal text, which outlined the authority in decision-making that every day public administrators may wield. In a nutshell, there is a certain level of discretion within which public administrators may enforce the policies, laws, etc., under their purview. Ideally, a staunch commitment to public service values will undergird all such decisions, and professional codes of ethics will keep such actions in check. Many professions – including those in the public sector – have adopted tailored codes of ethics, such as those outlined by the American Society for Public Administration (n.d.), International City/County Management Association (n.d.), or NASPA – Student Affairs Administrators in Higher Education (n.d.) (formerly known as the National Association of Student Personnel Administrators). Public servants are often faced with opportunities to exercise decision-making power that affects the community and individuals in their spheres of influence; therefore, it is necessary for public administrators to engage in professional reflection.

Law enforcement officers are an illustrative example of Lipsky's street-level bureaucrats. Suppose the posted speed limit for a city thoroughfare is 45 miles per hour. A police officer may choose to let someone slide who is driving 49 mph; that's their street-level bureaucrat decision-making authority. However, if the same driver starts drifting toward the center stripe, the police officer may opt to pull them over because they have an elevated concern that the driver may not be sober or may be distracted, such as texting while driving. The police officer has an obligation to act in the interest of the general public by prohibiting a dangerous driver from continuing to drive, thereby keeping other motorists and pedestrians safe from potential drunk-driving or other avoidable accidents.

The law enforcement officer in the above scenario must engage in *reflection-in-action* (Do I pull the driver over for speeding and driving erratically?); *reflection-on-action* (The decision to pull the driver over was worthwhile, based on their performance in the field sobriety or breathalyzer tests.); and perhaps even *reflection-for-action* (Based on patrol reports in recent months, this corridor has a higher rate of speeding drivers than other streets in town. We'll add a digital radar sign to remind drivers to watch their speed around this curve.).

Demonstrating Respect, Equity, and Fairness

Reflective leadership depends on communication. "Communication is the means by which understanding can be built." It is the vehicle that brings together diverse talents and directs all toward mutual goals, and propels members from the individual I's transforming to a capable we. Coherent collective action becomes possible with communication. Daily interactions are the foundational action for communication; however, communication is fundamentally a human endeavor that involves much more than the surface-level transmission of facts and information. The size of an organization does not matter; communication will always be the engagement of one human being with another.

Leaders who envision themselves above or apart from employees create an environment where communication will falter. Communication depends on shared values, beliefs, and attitudes; collectively, these components build the infrastructure that allow systematic approaches to continuous quality improvement. As noted in the NASPAA framework of public service values at the beginning of the chapter, necessary elements of reflective leadership include respect, equity, and fairness. Reflective leaders are responsible for creating communication-rich environments that support effective human systems where employees take ownership, engage in responsible risk taking, make independent decisions, further organizational goals, and work effectively in teams.

Case Study

A regional comprehensive state university recently conducted a climate survey to gauge faculty perspectives regarding assessment practices at the institution. Results from the survey revealed that nearly one-quarter of faculty members viewed assessment as a waste of time and resources. The survey indicated lower than anticipated perceptions of usefulness, as well as concerns among both non-tenure and tenure-track faculty regarding potential backlash or even punitive implications for providing results from assessments that did not result in stellar ratings. The university's new strategic plan prioritizes enhancing a culture of assessment across the institution, and the administration is worried that faculty are not taking the practice seriously.

Earlier in this chapter, we learned that accountability and transparency are critical components of public sector leadership. Transparency is tightly linked to access, and accountability breeds empowerment. By holding departments and faculty accountable to assessment practices, the university has the opportunity to empower its team with tools that can move the institution forward in a productive and positive manner, and the university's strategic focus on assessment necessitates increased transparency with its processes. Transparency is also important as the university aligns its objectives with accreditation expectations.

Considering a reflective approach toward assessment:

1. How might university leaders avoid having their assessment processes be seen as a potentially punitive means by which to judge faculty members' professional competency?
2. What steps can the university take to develop a culture of assessment as a formative, positive learning opportunity?

The university is at a critical crossroads, as they determine whether (and how) faculty are using assessment data to generate improvements at the course, departmental, college/school, and even institutional level. This process of closing the loop on learning assessment by identifying ways that the institution can use assessment data for improvement is an example of an important reflective practice that we will elaborate on in subsequent chapters (and extensive detail in Chapter 12), namely, reflection-for-action.

Conclusion

Now that we have explored how public service values tie into the notion of reflection as a professional practice, we will take what we have learned about these important values that are necessary for public sector leaders to commit to and uphold, and we will begin to explore what reflective practice looks like in the real world of the public sector workplace. This conscientious effort to retool the way we look at the scope and impact of our professional work is an element of reflection-for-action, which is one of three specific types of reflection that we will explore further in the next chapter.

References

American Psychological Association. (2015). In search of cultural competence. *Feature*, 46(3), 64. Retrieved from https://www.apa.org/monitor/2015/03/cultural-competence#:~:text=Cultural%20competence%20%E2%80%94%20loosely%20defined%20as,practice%20for%20some%2050%20years

American Society for Public Administration. (n.d.). *Advancing excellence in public service*. Retrieved from https://www.aspanet.org/ASPADocs/ASPA%20Code%20of%20Ethics-2013%20with%20Practices.pdf

Bowman, J., West, J., & Beck, M. (2010). *Achieving competencies in public service* (2nd ed.). New York: M. E. Sharpe. ISBN#978-0-7656-2348-5.

The Centers for Disease Control and Prevention. (n.d.). Retrieved from https://npin.cdc.gov/pages/cultural-competence

Chapin, R. K. (1995, July). Social policy development: The strengths perspective. *Social Work*, 40(4), 506–514. doi:10.1093/sw/40.4.

Eberhardt, J. L. (2019). *Biased: Uncovering the hidden prejudice that shapes what we see, think, and do*. New York: Viking Press.

FCC – Federal Communications Commission. (2011, July 18). Progress of the Open Government Directive at the Federal Communications Commission. Retrieved from https://www.fcc.gov/general/open-government-directive

Freeman, L. C. (2008). Establishing effective advising practices to influence student learning and success. *Peer Review*, 10(1), 12.

IACP – International Association of Chiefs of Police. (n.d.). Code of Ethics. Retrieved from https://www.theiacp.org/resources/law-enforcement-code-of-ethics#

International Association of Chiefs of Police. (n.d.). Retrieved from https://www.theiacp.org/resources/policy-center-resource/standards-of-conduct

International City/County Management Association. (n.d.). Retrieved from https://icma.org/icma-code-ethics

Karrick, P. M. (2016). Sorting it out: Cultural competency and healthcare literacy in the world today. *Nursing Science Quarterly*, 29(2), 120–121. doi:10.1177/0894318416630105.

KU SSW – University of Kansas School of Social Welfare. (n.d.). Retrieved from https://socwel.ku.edu/strengths-perspective

Lipsky, M. (2010). *Street-level bureaucracy: Dilemmas of the individual in public services*. New York: Russell Sage Foundation.

NASPA – Student Affairs Administrators in Higher Education. (n.d.). Retrieved from https://www.naspa.org/division/professional-standards-division

NASPAA – Network of Schools of Public Policy, Affairs, and Administration. (n.d.-a) Standard 5. Standard 5 Matching Operations with the Mission: Student Learning, p. 8. https://www.naspaa.org/sites/default/files/docs/2019-11/NASPAA%20Accreditation%20Standards%20-%202019%20FINAL%20with%20rationale.pdf

NASPAA – Network of Schools of Public Policy, Affairs, and Administration. (n.d.-b). Preconditions. *Preconditions for Accreditation Review*, p. 2. https://www.naspaa.org/sites/default/files/docs/2019-11/NASPAA%20Accreditation%20Standards%20-%202019%20FINAL%20with%20rationale.pdf

NASPAA – Network of Schools of Public Policy, Affairs, and Administration. (n.d.-c). *Revised accreditation standards*. Retrieved from https://www.naspaa.org/revised-naspaa-accreditation-standards

Pearson, T. A. (2019). "After a neutral and impartial investigation…": Implicit bias in internal workplace investigations (Dissertation). Rossier School of Education, University of Southern California, p. 25.

Saleeby, D. (2002). *The strengths perspective in social work practice* (3rd ed.). Boston, MA: Pearson.

Schein, E. (2010). *Organizational culture and leadership*. San Francisco, CA: Jossey-Bass.

Serpas, R. W. (n.d.) Beyond CompStat: Accountability-driven leadership. *Police Chief Magazine*. Retrieved from https://www.policechiefmagazine.org/beyond-compstat-accountability/

Thomas Bernard, W., & Moriah, J. (2007). Cultural competency: An individual or institutional responsibility? *Canadian Social Work Review/Revue Canadienne De Service Social*, *24*(1), 81–92. Retrieved from http://www.jstor.org/stable/41669863

Triolo, P. (2012). Creating cultures of excellence: Transforming organizations. In G. Sherwood & J. Barnsteiner (Eds.), *Quality and safety in nursing: A competency approach to improving outcomes* (pp. 305–322). Hoboken, NJ: Wiley-Blackwell.

Winters, M.-F. (2020). *Inclusive conversations*. Oakland, CA: Berrett-Koehler Publishers.

3
REFLECTION AS GOOD PRACTICE

Reflection as a learning tool has been embraced in educational circles for some time, as described in the first chapter. Reflection serves as an infrastructural component of leadership. However, reflection should not merely be considered a stage in a cycle of experiential learning; it is a critical practice that ought to be implemented throughout the curriculum, as well as beyond graduation and into the profession itself. Heifetz, Grashow, and Linsky (2002) wrote about the challenge of reflection and leadership using the metaphor of the balcony and the dance floor. Noting "self reflection does not come naturally," they point out the importance of practicing taking a balcony perspective on events-viewing the meeting or event from a bird's eye perspective to better see patterns or understand what is going on (Heifetz et al., 2002, p. 51). Nevertheless, if one wants to impact what is in progress, they have to visit the dance floor. Reflection should not be considered as value added, its primary service is as a foundational component of leadership/development. This chapter will build upon the public service values discussion from the previous chapter and consider how reflection as a professional practice within the workplace is a key element to becoming an effective public administrator.

From Public Service Values to Curriculum and Beyond

Svara and Baizhanov (2019) categorized the implementation of public service values within educational programs into three buckets: identification, integration, and activation. They begin with the call to *identify* public service values within the educational program by explicitly including values verbiage in the mission statement and program competencies. In other words, does the mission statement itself include explicit mention of public service values, and

DOI: 10.4324/9781003270775-5

do the program's learning objectives reflect the same values? Next, programs need to *integrate* key values into courses across the curriculum. Do the syllabi, assignments, readings, and class activities build upon public service values?

Reflection-in-action provides lead administrators with an opportunity to examine mission fit goals and priorities, promoting efficient communication. Employees are able to use reflection to match their fit within the mission and what skill they must develop to enhance their mission fit development. Reflection-in-action limits the distortion of information from sender to receiver therefore, improvising common shared organization development.

Sherwood and Horton-Deutsch (2015) add that reflection applies theory from all ways of knowing and learning as an extension of evidence-based practices and research. Finally, programs can *activate* these important values by drawing a connection between the curriculum, interdisciplinary studies, activities, and professional codes of ethics. Are public administration graduates familiar with the codes of ethics for their specific fields and the profession, at large?

> **MIRROR MOMENT**
>
> Take a moment to look up the code of ethics for your profession (typically via a professional organization such as NASPAA, ICMA, etc.) or the network affiliated with your chosen field of study. What strikes you as instantly applicable in your work or educational setting? What aspect(s) of the code of ethics sound like areas of improvement at the organizational/institutional level? What about areas that you would like to enhance, personally?

Identification, integration, and activation are important steps in developing effective public administration educational programs, but the process for applying public service values as described by Svara and Bizhanov (2019) also overlaps with three types of reflection: *reflection-in-action*, *reflection-on-action*, and *reflection-for-action*. Next, we will consider each of these steps individually as they relate to specific types of reflection, so we can begin to make the connection between theory and practice in the real world (Figure 3.1).

Reflection-in-Action

Schön (1983) is widely credited with introducing the concept of reflection into the workforce through his 1983 text, which placed particular emphasis on how professionals in the fields of engineering, architecture, management, psychotherapy, and town planning successfully solved problems on the fly. He referred to this professional skill as *reflection-in-action*. This step represents

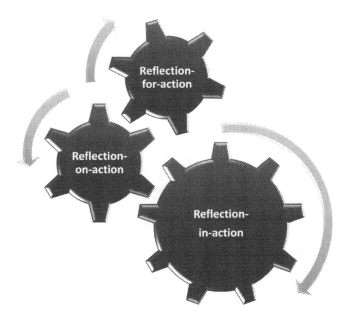

FIGURE 3.1 Three types of reflective practice

the improvisational aspect of reflection; it involves being in the moment and thinking while doing. A professional uses reflection-in-action to identify a perceived problem as a situation unfolds. Put in other words, reflection-in-action happens in real time and is an opportunity to consider what is happening, and what you are doing in the midst of the circumstance.

It is this process of reflection-in-action that provides a central platform for individuals to address activities of uncertainty, instability, uniqueness, and conflict in the moment of a group meeting or within an individual setting. Reflection-in-action is integral for leaders to fully develop skills and dispositions. Professionals are encouraged to think through what they are doing and provide themselves with critique. The critically reflective professional will want to assess progress toward goals and then modify behaviors to meet goals. Reflection provides essential opportunities for identifying and questioning assumptions, beliefs, and values.

Identification Step

Taking Svara and Baizhanov's (2019) *identification* stage beyond the classroom and into the public sector workforce, we might start by asking whether the agency's mission statement is a pervasive, inclusive element in the day-to-day operations of the organization. Are employees educated on the organization's purpose as an essential component of onboarding? If employees are asked what purpose the agency serves, could they convey a consistent message? Whether an agency has its sights on an external audit exercise or a higher education institution is facing reaccreditation, the question of mission fit is critical for organizations to grapple with as they reflect upon who and what they aim to become. When confronted with unanticipated concerns related to mission and vision (either positive or negative), reflective leaders examine the possible actions and outcomes, embracing the problem in an effort to move beyond existing conceptions. The focus of reflection-in-action may include systems, patterns, behaviors, situations, or a specific problem (Volpe White, Guthrie, & Torres, 2019).

Reflection-on-Action

Reflection-on-action deals with what you learned through the situation. This type of learning does not happen by accident; it involves evaluating expectations, observing impacts, and even questioning the status quo. As Ash and Clayton (2009) explain, "A critical reflection process that generates, deepens, and documents learning does not occur automatically—rather, it must be carefully and intentionally designed" (p. 28). Like much of the current academic literature on the topic of reflective practice, Ash and Clayton's research centers on educational settings. However, we can extract important principles to apply for practitioners in the public sphere, be it within education, criminal justice, local/state/regional/federal government, nonprofit organizations, or a myriad of other public service professions.

Reflection-on-action occurs when an individual integrates their professional skills and knowledge base to better understand how to fix the issue at hand. Constructively critical and purposeful reflection-on-action can become an important component of a public administrator's professional toolbox. This mode of reflection is presented primarily as an analytical exercise resulting in new perspectives on experiences, changes in behavior, and commitments to action. Through reflection-on-action, leaders consciously return to past experiences, reevaluating them and analyzing what they could have done differently in preparation to implement these new strategies (Merriam, Caffarella, and Baumgartner 2007). This forward-thinking final step segues into reflection-for-action, which we will explore in more depth below.

Integration Step

With regard to the *integration* component of Svara and Baizhanov's (2019) incorporation of public service values, does the organization's mission statement drive decision-making at the agency level? Is the strategic plan merely a document on a shelf to be dusted off prior to the next audit or accreditation cycle, or does it actively inform processes and procedures as a regular practice? In the context of the public and nonprofit sector, an organization's mission statement ought to be the foundation for any initiative, and every endeavor of the organization needs to circle back to how it contributes to fulfilling its strategic plan. In order to truly integrate public service values into the core of the organization, its mission statement and strategic plan should be the focal point for every level of decision-making within the organization.

> **MIRROR MOMENT**
>
> What is the current strategic plan at your organization/agency/institution? Is it up to date? (Were you aware of it before this exercise?) Skim through the document and identify the key components of the plan. Can you spot any of Svara and Baizhanov's public service values within the document? What areas are lacking, if any?

Reflection-for-Action

Reflection-for-action involves thinking beyond the current situation or encounter, anticipating future actions or plans leading toward possible improvements based on prior experience. Reflection-for-action is concerned with what you could do in similar scenarios in the future. Olteanu (2016) points out that reflection-for-action is connected to the intended objective of learning (a planning stage) which refers to the content that students should learn and that is to be covered in the classroom. (Coulson and Harvey (2013) actually recommend implementing this step upfront in educational scenarios, with the intention of preparing students to engage in experiential learning activities. For the present discussion, however, we will place this phase as the final step toward future planning for the professional public servant.)

Fogarty and Pete (2020) note the importance of implementing this process in the educational setting: "Reflection is as natural as dreaming and imagining. Yet, for a number of years, this skill set of reflective thinking–forecasting, hypothesizing in our planning, examining, determining our ongoing progress, and appraising and evaluating the results of what we have done–has most definitely been a mystery of implementation in our classrooms" (p. xi). Throughout this text, the authors aim to link the importance of reflective practice as a learning tool in educational settings with reflection as a professional practice for ongoing development and continuous improvement. Both are crucial for the future of the broader field of public administration.

In the reflection-for-action process, the administrator will make active, strategic changes necessary to address the concern systematically. Transformative change can be evident in the reflection-for-action stage. Here is where the relationship between reflection-in-action and reflection-on-action exist. Prior experience plays a major role in the development of future planning for change within reflection-for-action. Additionally, reflection-for-action is affixed to enacting the concept of learning and to the engaged objective of learning what is possible to experience with the environment of strategic planning and continuous quality improvement. This is where long-term change begins to take root.

Activation Step

The reflection-for-action step dovetails with Svara and Baizhanov's (2019) *activation* stage of meshing public service values with educational practice. Are employees encouraged to become active members of professional organizations and have access to conferences and other professional development opportunities? Does the agency look to peer organizations in terms of best practices, with an eye toward continuous improvement? Is the notion of change looked at with contempt or anticipation within the agency? If an organization is to embrace a growth mindset, then it cannot continue to operate in business-as-usual mode. The agency and its people need to be open to innovative ideas, trying new ways of doing things, as well as implementing new systems and processes. Change can be a challenge, but it is the only way to grow.

Context of Reflection Types within Public Administration

Next, we will take a closer look at the three types of reflection within a public administration context:

1. *Reflection-in-action* could be an academic dean serving on a search committee who glances around the conference table at an all-white panel and recommends the group that invite more people representing diverse and varying perspectives to the job search.
2. *Reflection-on-action* looks like the dean attending a workshop on implicit bias because she realizes that creating a climate of inclusivity throughout the college means more than just diversifying candidate pools.
3. *Reflection-for-action* means the dean returns from the workshop and evaluates the college's current strategic plan to see how well it incorporates equity and inclusion as foundational goals, then sets the wheels in motion to implement new, college-wide diversity objectives by convening a steering committee of varied stakeholders.

> **MIRROR MOMENT**
>
> Thinking of your current agency or institution, select an individual position or department and brainstorm how you would describe the three types of reflection in action. What would it look like for this person or unit to implement reflective practice in the moment, in retrospect, and for future planning purposes?

Application of Reflection within the Public Sector

Returning to the three categories of identification, integration, and activation, we can evaluate the dean's reflection steps further. In the *reflection-in-action* phase, she identified a problem – namely, a lack of diversity on the search committee. She used the *reflection-on-action* stage to implement new training for herself and others, so they can be on the same page going forward. By activating her plan through *reflection-for-action*, she helped create a strategic plan and evaluation tool leading to a stronger system to not only address the current problem, but also aim to avoid similar situations in the future.

Reflection as a professional practice does not have to be complicated, but it should entail a conscientious and consistent effort. However, a sense of efficacy can be gained by engaging in a systematic process of reflecting on expectations and practice, making adjustments, and taking careful note of improvements in beliefs, practices, and building community. This type of reflection involves more than journaling or keeping a diary of the day's events. We will explore more pragmatic steps in later chapters; for now, let us consider the merits of reflection as it relates to professions in the public sector. To echo Eyler, Giles, and Schmiede (1996), reflection "need not be a difficult process, but it does need to be a purposeful and strategic process" (p. 16). While their text on *Reflection in Service Learning* centered on a study regarding experiential education, the authors offered some valuable insights that could translate to the public workforce. Reflection is a strategic, systematic process of thinking about actions and within a knowledge base; it is learning from experience by considering reframing to develop further responses or actions (Sherwood & Horton-Deutsch, 2015).

Critical Reflection

For starters, Eyler et al. (1996) noted that students who were not exposed to reflective practice with a critical thinking lens were most likely to view their experiences with emphasis on "... the personal and the empathetic dimensions of the experience," whereas students who engaged in structured, critical reflection tended to exhibit "… a better sense of application of ideas to social problems and a transformed understanding of the problem and issues surrounding it" (p. 16).

Scaled to the professional experience, we might anticipate that public administrators who engage in purposeful reflection might be more likely to be open to changes that address systemic problems. To be clear, critical reflection is much more than a purely cognitive process of analysis and speculation; instead, critical reflection is an artistic process. It is intuitive, improvisational, and creative. Practitioners make confident judgments regarding appropriate responses to situations and problems for which no explicit rationale has been developed.

The correlation warrants further study, but for the present discussion, let us explore Eyler, Giles, and Schmiede's four principles of reflection from the lens of a public administrator and see what we can apply from the classroom perspective into the workplace:

1. Continuous Reflection: In their study of students engaged in a service learning experience, Eyler, Giles, and Schmiede found that "… critical reflection must be an ongoing part …" (p. 10) of the students' experiences, and that continuity throughout the duration of the experience (prior to, during, and afterward) is also important to a well-rounded experiential learning activity (p. 17). When reflection is considered a long-term component of a learning activity, it becomes a natural focal point of the overarching experience, which meshes with Svara and Baizhanov's (2019) *identification* stage of applying public service values. (Consider the discussion previously about incorporating the organization's mission statement into day-to-day practice; likewise, if critical reflection is valued as an ongoing professional exercise, then it can become part of one's habitual practice.) When intentional reflection is built into a public administrator's professional goals, it can become second nature to engage in reflection-in-action as a matter of course.
2. Connected Reflection: As we discussed in Chapter 1 with regard to the linkage between theory and practice, reflection helps connect service/work with the theories behind our actions. Reflection-on-action, then, becomes the application component to put theories into practice. Eyler, Giles, and Schmiede describe connected reflection as helping students "… illustrate theories and concepts," which gives students a broader perspective of their work in the context of greater society (p. 18). Similarly, the integration phase from Svara and Baizhanov (2019) helps bring big picture goals to a local, deliverable level. In the context of professional application, connected reflection could help a public administrator see the broader implications of their day-to-day work by putting them in touch with both the *what* and *why* of their duties.

3. Challenging Reflection: This step makes the segue from introspection to critical thinking by prodding individuals with intervention in the form of challenging questions and ideas. Translating this phase to the professional workforce, we can consider the shift from reflection-on-action to reflection-for-action through intervention and problem solving. In any given situation, public administrators might ask themselves to explore alternative explanations for scenarios and question their initial presumptions or perceptions.
4. Contextualized Reflection: In this phase, Eyler, Giles, and Schmiede encourage students to explore the community context of their service learning activity, in order to draw a meaningful "... synthesis between thinking and doing" (p. 20). Extended to the professional setting, we might consider both reflection-for-action and the activation phase as contextual elements of reflection. As aforementioned, reflection-for-action is a forward-thinking endeavor, with an eye toward future decision-making. Activation is where the rubber meets the road, so to speak: Is the reflection effort applicable to a real-world scenario, present or prospective?

Case Study

A state university recently instituted a new mission and vision statement in an effort to move the university forward to address a changing college culture and economic climate. During the change process a number of teams were formed to include students, staff, faculty, support staff, and community stakeholders. University administrators at the Deans level or higher were assigned to lead the various teams. The university hired consultants to outline the process. The active engagement with the community included the use of appreciative inquiry, storyboarding, and a review of old mission statements and ten years of financial data.

The decision to rewrite the college mission and vision is challenging for everyone. There were times when groups disbursed due to arguments, hurt feelings, and decisions that were not inclusive of the community and stakeholders served by the university. Employees questioned mission fit and community stakeholders were not convinced that diversity and inclusion were high on the university's priorities within its new direction.

The decision to pursue a new mission and vision was challenging for the university President and its Board of Trustees. In its 75 years of existence the mission and vision had never changed. The mission never addressed fit and administrative and board decisions were made without consideration of the mission or its community stakeholders. The community often encouraged students to seek postsecondary education elsewhere. Support from local community organizations and businesses started to diminish. So, addressing the mission, vision, and fit was necessary to reestablish its relationship with a variety of communities, and businesses. The university was presented with a number of high-risk obstacles to conquer.

Upper-level administrators lacked the ability to mobilize key stakeholders. The consultants were puzzled by the limited focus of the executive leadership team. The consultants made the ultimate decision to disband all established teams in an effort to help the executive cabinet regroup and refocus on why the university exists. This action was selected to review university values and practices within the mission before teams could continue their work. Activations and sustainability of values and practices within departments did not exist. This led to distrust and apprehension by students, faculty, staff, and the community. There was limited thinking beyond current situations. Planning was on a year-to-year basis. There was no strategic plan.

Now, having decided to support the consultant's direction and strategy, the executive team recalled why they were hired and their commitment to serve students, faculty, and community stakeholders. As a leadership team there were apprehensions about inclusion and diversity. This was a product of the composition of the executive team. The team lacked any diversity and the Board exhibited the same composition. The university's emphasis on men in leadership positions was a major obstacle.

The process of rewriting the university mission and vision presented major concerns for all involved. Consultants and employees grappled with being at the forefront of major change. They believed the university was of value to the community and its stakeholders. They (employees, students, and stakeholders) realized their perspectives aligned with the development of a change agenda. There was support for the university to engage a mission, vision, and strategic plan that embraced a new direction that was diverse and inclusive of all.

The President, executive team, and the Board of Trustees felt it was for change. After 75 years of existence leadership forced itself to challenge existing beliefs, values, practices, and norms. In other words, without change and redevelopment the future of the university would be limited.

Discussion Questions

1. Discuss and define an outline of an initial plan the consultants can deploy using reflective practice.
2. In your opinion, what would reflection-in-action demonstrate in the first meeting of the executive team and the board of trustees? Identify and list three possible outcomes.

3. How would you use the data and information acquired during the appreciative inquiry and storyboarding sessions to engage community stakeholders in a reflection-for-action conversation with the consultants? What role does critical reflection play in this scenario?

Conclusion

The practice of reflection can be of major importance to leaders. The question is, how do leaders, new and experienced, create a disposition for an ongoing practice of reflection? Experiential learning serves as an important tool for moving from hindsight to reflection. Gonzalez Sullivan and Aalsburg Wiessner (2010) advise leaders/learners to develop a priority toward reflection as a means for constructing needed perspectives from daily experiences to their work context and personal and professional lives. Without reflection it is easy to repeat past mistakes or fail to repeat approaches that were ineffective in previous situations (p. 43). Continuous development of reflective practice is a vital necessary component of adopting a lifelong habit and disposition for reflection. Sustainable change does not occur without a systematic approach to development and implementation. Change is based on prior experience with learning and organizational environments, using reflective practices and actions to achieve concepts that are grounded leading to values, beliefs, and behaviors that move the organization forward.

References

Ash, S. L., & Clayton, P. H. (2009). Generating, deepening, and documenting learning: The power of critical reflection in applied learning. *Journal of Applied Learning in Higher Education*, 1, 25–48.

Coulson, D., & Harvey, M. (2013). Scaffolding student reflection for experience-based learning: A framework. *Teaching in Higher Education*, 18(4), 401–413. doi:10.1080/13562517.2012.752726.

Eyler, J., Giles, D. E., & Schmiede, A. (1996) *A Practitioner's guide to reflection in service learning: Student voices & reflections*. Nashville, TN: Vanderbilt University Press, p. 16.

Fogarty, R. J., & Pete, B. M. (2020). *Metacognition: The neglected skill set for empowering students, revised edition (your planning guide to teaching mindful, reflective, proficient thinkers and problem solvers)*. Solution Tree. *ProQuest Ebook Central*. Retrieved from https://ebookcentral.proquest.com/lib/fhsu/detail.action?docID=6215730

González Sullivan, L., & Aalsburg Wiessner, C. (2010). Learning to be reflective leaders: A case study from NCCHC Hispanic leadership fellows program. *New Directions for Community Colleges*, 149, 41–49.

Heifetz, R., Grashow, A., & Linsky, M. (2009). *The practice of adaptive leadership: Tools and tactics for changing your organization and the world*. Boston, MA: Harvard Business Press.

Olteanu, C. (2016). Reflection-for-action and the choice or design of examples in the teaching of mathematics. *Mathematics Education Research Journal, 29*, 349–367. doi:10.1007/s13394-017-211-9.

Schön, D. (1983). *The reflective practitioner: How professionals think in action*. New York: Basic Books.

Sherwood, G. D., & Horton-Deutsch, S. (2015). *Reflective organizations*. Indianapolis, IN: Sigma Theta Tau International.

Svara, J. H., & Baizhanov, S. (2019). Public service values in NASPAA programs: Identification, integration, and activation. *Journal of Public Affairs Education, 25*(1), 73–92. doi:10.1080/15236803.2018.1454761.

Volpe White, J. M., Guthrie, K. L., & Torres, M. (2019). *Thinking to transform reflection in leadership learning*. Charlotte, NC: Information Age Publishing.

PART II
Tools for Reflection

4
REFLECTION AS HINDSIGHT

Beyond Constraints: Reflection and Lifelong Learning

Reflection provides a strategy for new learning; it is a means for linking technical and intuitive knowledge and gives opportunities to examine practices that may be constrained by institutional structures. Put another way, the reflective practice compels us to engage in both cognitive and affective responses to stimuli around us. A cognitive perspective means that we gain insight into others' thought processes and belief systems; however, viewing others through an affective lens allows us to better understand the emotional basis for their actions (Healey & Grossman, 2018).

Within educational and workplace settings, reflection can help us examine the multiple vantage points necessary to promote interactions with learners and colleagues. Practitioners should embrace the approachability of reflective practice for the inclusivity of all learners, colleagues, and clients. White, Guthrie, and Torres (2017) explain that it is important for each of us to process both cognitive and affective responses to experiences in order to enhance development and understanding of social, political, educational, and economic structures during the lifelong learning process.

> **MIRROR MOMENT**
>
> Theoretical foundations are a strength within reflective practice, as we discussed in Chapter 1. How would the use of theory assist the deployment of reflection-on-action as you develop strategies for interacting with others

DOI: 10.4324/9781003270775-7

> in a way that supports transparent and holistic dialogue? Based on what you've learned so far, how can you approach your colleagues, classmates, and/or clients from both a cognitive and an affective angle?

Reflective practice is an important theme in transforming education and business structures. However, a reorganization process must first embrace the theory of transformative learning (see Chapter 1). The important steps of reflection-in-action, on-action, and for-action are limited without a process of transformative learning, which boils down to a change in the way we see ourselves, the organization, and the stakeholders our agencies serve. Our goal should be fulfilling the organizational mission and framing new pathways, goals, and actions to create a reflective organization that is inclusive of lifelong, reflective engagement that creates continuous learning and improvement.

As practitioners and lifelong learners, we must continuously reflect on questions that encourage growth of self, organizations, and stakeholders. For instance, let us consider the following prompts about our work in the public sector:

1. How might we more fully integrate our organizational mission, vision, standards, and goals into our own roles, as well as the broader agency/institution?
2. What changes are necessary to embrace current and prospective internal and external stakeholders?
3. What are some ways we could integrate reflective practice into quality and growth opportunities, with an eye toward transforming the organization and employees?

As discussed in previous chapters, the core principles of reflective practice dovetail closely with experiential learning theory. Boud, Keogh, and Walker (1985) explain that tightening the connection between an educational activity and subsequent reflection on the experience is key to boosting the overall process of learning. (Indeed, this intersection between learning and reflection is the premise of experiential education. However, throughout this text, we are seeking to show the reader that reflection is an all-encompassing foundation for lifelong learning and professional development, not merely a stage in the educational process.)

In order to develop as lifelong learners, we need to adapt new insights and couple them with activity-based reinforcement in order to enhance our learning curves. In this manner, reflection and experience are in sync and continue to build upon each other as we encounter new lessons and learning opportunities throughout our lives. Consider, for example, the early days of distance education through correspondence courses. The process was linear, where materials were sent (or made available) to students to study independently, then return to the instructor to be graded and earn credit for the class. Nowadays, effective online education has morphed into a much more holistic approach to the students' experiences. Students expect to be engaged on a personal level in their virtual classes, not only through discussion boards but also through interactive activities, tools, and assignments.

Reflection is not something that can be performed once and retired. It is focused on personal growth, team development, experiences, theories, and organization – not only in the moment of the learning experience but also over time. The lifelong learning process drives exploration, knowledge transfer, growth, and improvement by paying attention to mission, vision, beliefs, and values. This cyclical learning process occurs while also inspiring individuals and organizations to embrace a change agenda. After all, growth inherently involves change. We will discuss the importance of a broadened worldview in more detail in Chapter 8, but it correlates with the notion of growth and change: Our lived experiences (along with our willingness to learn from others) dictate the worldview through which we operate. If we truly aspire to become lifelong learners, then we must also embrace the idea of stretching our worldview as we go along.

The Transformational Power of Reflection

Cyclical reflection allows for significant appreciation of how meaning is being expressed by participants during *and* after situations occur. As an ongoing activity, reflection-in-action and on-action, as well as for-action after the fact, can become an ecological rather than ego-logical practice. In nature, an ecosystem depends on sunlight, water, plants, organisms, and soil in balanced measure. If any one component of the ecosystem is removed or hindered, the whole system is endangered. Likewise, the three types of reflective practice could be considered an ecosystem, of sorts, for how we grow and function as lifelong learners. When reflective practice becomes part of one's overall ecosystem of operations, individuals and teams are free to gather what emerges from the collision of different perspectives, rather than maintaining preconceived personal and/or professional agendas.

The mission-critical concepts of experience and transformation provide opportunities to engage in reflection as an actionable practice in the moment, rather than merely a consideration in hindsight. Acting in a transformation mindset requires visionary thinking, as well as an approach to change that energizes and stimulates people, teams, and eventually even communities to consider new designs and processes over the status quo. Outcomes of this approach may include competencies, such as strategic planning, innovation, thinking analytically, team building, fiscal soundness, and inclusive participation by various stakeholders. In other words, a transformation perspective is forward-thinking with an eye toward accomplishing future goals (McGoff, 2011).

As we explored in Chapter 1, transformative learning also teaches us to recognize and evaluate how we can couple knowledge gained through reflective practice with critical thinking, which then allows us to make judgment calls and continually assess how to adapt to situations during seasons of change. Transformative learning is more than acquiring new knowledge; it includes critical reflection to question assumptions, values, and perspectives in making decisions and choices in daily work (Sherwood & Horton-Deutsch, 2015). While we will discuss the importance of developing critical thinking skills in an educational setting more in Chapter 12, these techniques are certainly not limited to the classroom. They can be implemented in the workplace and even everyday interactions with others. One example related to questioning assumptions might involve second-guessing an opinion that someone else delivered as a fact and making the time to conduct your own research on the topic. Using critical reflection practices to better understand one's own values and perspectives might mean listening to a podcast or seeking out a book written by an author from an underrepresented demographic to learn from their vantage point.

Reflective practitioners engage in a process of becoming critically aware of how and why our assumptions about the world in which we operate have come to constrain the way we see ourselves and our relationships. Transformative learning, in turn, helps develop a critical thinking mindset by raising questions about assumptions and current knowledge. Both concepts hinge on the willingness and ability to change. The base is inquiry and engagement; it is characterized by openness to improvement, analysis of what happens within situations, and adjustment to each new scenario, based on knowledge acquisition, development, and incorporation of new information.

Sherwood and Horton-Deutsch (2015) note that experience is the integral part of transformative learning, which separates experiential learning (flexible in nature, with no specific ending point) from cognitive learning (acquiring and manipulating information). Qutoshi (2018) holds that this experience piece is critical because transformation involves a deeper level of change that could lead to a paradigm shift in thinking, believing, and doing as a process of continuous professional development. Thus, transformation is linked with the concept of continuous improvement through critical reflection, and that is more sustainable than a surface level change embedded in a reformative agenda.

To illustrate this concept of transformation as a phase beyond experience and cognitive understanding, we can look at the sizable increase in gym memberships after the beginning of a new calendar year. Individuals cognitively know that they need to make healthier lifestyle choices, and they may even set specific weight loss goals or a New Year's Resolution to run a marathon in the coming year. These well-meaning people jump onto the bandwagon experience and sign up for a membership at a local fitness center. If all we are seeking is evidence that a change began, then that would be the end of the story. However, evidence shows year after year that many of the newcomers in January aren't still committed to attending the gym come February, much less as the months pass by. Those who undergo a truly transformative experience are those who develop an altered frame of mind that prioritizes the entire wellness journey as a fresh perspective on their lives. They know that continuing to behave and think in the same way they have been will not yield new, improved results.

Taking this notion of transformative learning and reflective practice beyond the individual's personal experience and applying it into the public sector workplace, consider that the primary focus of Continuous Quality Improvement (CQI) is to impact the performance of companies (for profit and non-profit) for improvement. The development of enterprise depends on identifying needs of stakeholders and offering solutions with adjustments to meet expectations as needs and goals evolve. Appropriate strategies to meet stakeholder expectations require engagement to design, develop, and implement, mission, goals, values, and beliefs.

Reflective practice and transformation are embedded into each step of the CQI process that a team utilizes. Objectives of the organization become achievable by using reflection tools to capitalize on human resources, financial and logistical resources, professionalism, responsibility, and innovation. By implementing transformative learning, reflective leaders are able to engage in behaviors that direct and inspire efforts toward fulfilling organizational goals. As explained by Thy Jensen and Ladegaard Bro (2018), reflective leaders accomplish these quality-centered objectives by articulating a vision that raises awareness to the importance of organizational values, mission, and outcomes.

Transformation as an action-oriented tool assists with the adjustment and rethinking of traditional frames of references (habits, values, and beliefs) and encourages the examination of their fit in a modern, inclusive work environment. This practice also generates ideas and concepts that justify and guide actions of individuals and teams on a continuous improvement journey. Transformative actions within reflective practice can free individuals and team members to consider, examine, and accept purposes, values, and ideas of community stakeholders. Mezirow (2000) observed transformation in our habits of mind may be sudden and dramatic (epochal), or they may be slower, incremental changes in our points of view (meaning schemes), which eventually leads to a change in our habits of mind (meaning perspective).

Epochal transformation often has influential and uniquely significant moments that lead to monumental adjustment. The election of Barack Obama as the President of the United States could be considered an epochal transformation. The election was unexpected, yet it created a transformational existence for the United State and the world. Incremental transformation is considered an adjustment of refinement that modifies a process or action. Often a series of small steps taking place over a long period of time. Both epochal and incremental progress can lead to an individual, group, team, or organization changing its attitude, point of view, or direction.

> **MIRROR MOMENT**
>
> Transformational learning engages critical reflection to question perspectives and decisions. What barriers do you feel are present with the use of transformational learning? What elements must be present to implement a change agenda using transformational learning?

Reflection Is More Than a To-Do List

Reflection as an active process neither consists solely of activities incorporated into curricular and co-curricular experiences, nor is reflection purely a theoretical exercise or examination. The richness of reflection for practitioners/learners lies in pairing experiences with theory-driven reflections to facilitate learning and development. White et al. (2017) state that there are situations where reflection is often reduced to activities without a broader understanding of the undergirding theory (p. 32). This is an anomaly that causes harm to the future development of reflective practice (Figure 4.1).

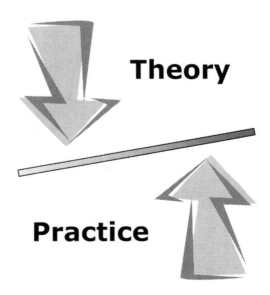

FIGURE 4.1 Balancing theory and practice

Preparedness to think critically and engage others in reflection upon activities, values, beliefs, and outcomes is a central tenet of reflective practice, while working in the moment (reflection-in-action), reviewing after the fact (reflection-on-action), or planning for the future (reflection-for-action). In this regard, reflective practice can be considered to incorporate critical thinking. There is a deliberate course of action(s) involving a critical dimension producing judgment(s), decision(s), and change based on review of criteria and results. Reflective interventions within a group are often inclusive of dialogue, a review of literature or best practices, data analysis, benchmarking, and inquiry. The practice involves engagements within a department, division, or the entire enterprise, often leading toward change or process improvements as an outcome. The use of critical thinking skills, to establish hypotheses, finding criteria, and identifying assumptions and implications are critical ingredients between team members supported by attitudes of openness, trust, respect, and honesty.

Reflection serves as a response to an experience. According to Boud et al. (1985), reflection is an important human activity in which people recapture their experience, think about it, mull it over, and evaluate it. It is this working experience that is important in learning: It is an expressed action inclusive of more than thinking, like how experiential education is learning but through hands-on application than merely rote memory. Reflection means more than checking off a to-do list, as discussed in Chapter 1; instead, reflective practice engages us on an intellectual and even emotional level.

Within the process of reflective practice, practitioners may encounter feelings and emotions with regard to their and others' work that have influence on what is being done and how it is accomplished. These subjective variables like feelings and emotion have the potential to derail a reflective process, and practitioners or leaders of a reflective activity need to address visible and invisible variables. According to Sze Goh (2019), workers can explore the assumptions that frame their understanding of the problems and search for responses to problems through reflective practice. Lifelong learning that incorporates reflective practice involves the inclusion of shared efforts, with emphasis on organizational/team intent rather than singular aspiration. The process requires joint efforts and not isolated actions from team and institutional intentions. Collective reflective practice can tend to concentrate on a specific context, there is a tendency to overlook the effects of previous learning, present learning, or future learning, and these elements should not be omitted. Efforts to confront these limitations require an individual to act, if practitioners are to influence ongoing and future practices within their agencies and organizations.

Practitioners must embrace the concept of a community to enable shared experiences that can strengthen each step within the reflective process. The reality of a constructive reflection comes to fruition as participants from similar or dissimilar teams join together to examine issues important for performance improvements. The importance of collective reflection is to provoke teams that are thinking about institutional concerns in an effort to develop outcomes that support development of improved processes, goals, values, and policies that provide stakeholders with the capacity and tools to take care of current and future challenges.

Working is a shared learning process that has the ability to create learning dialogue, providing constructive information that individual practitioners may have forgotten or overlooked. Practitioners participating in team reflection are providing information, ideas are being examined and challenged, and collectively, they are facilitating an environment that encourages contribution to analysis and process improvements. Practitioners encounter experiences and learn within the reflective process, individually and through team interactions. Although reflection can be a collective activity, it begins from the individual's personal and professional experiences to equip individuals with a sense of their own professional identity in the context of changing conditions that can produce a change in organizational process, practice, and conditions.

The Emotional Complexity of Reflection

The reflective process is complex: It incorporates feelings and cognition closely; both are interrelated, and interactive emotion is central to reflective processes. Emotions can influence knowledge, influence the process of reflection, or arise from the process of reflection. Reflection used in individual, team, or organizational contexts must cultivate interactive sharing of opinions, seeking reactions, stimulation of team engagement, observation, and assessment. The process of reflection requires support within the individual, team, or collective organizational construction (including values, beliefs, and procedures). Feelings, emotions, and cognition are challenged and disconnected without opportunities to establish connections and dialogue.

The reflective process can energize the creation of new ideas, while at the same time developing practices that encourage adjustments made in real time as agendas change (Hilden & Tikkamäki, 2013). In other words, reflection is not studied as a hidden mental process, but instead, as a visible practice directed at past, present, and/or future objectives. Reflective practice is an important ingredient in mental modeling, vision-sharing, team learning, systems thinking, and mastering one's personal self. Introspection can be identified as a cognitive reflective process assisting as a bridge between experience and learning. This link establishes an active and steadfast process of exploration and inquiry that supports awareness of assumptions influencing individual actions, thinking, and feelings.

> **MIRROR MOMENT**
>
> A colleague introduces a radical new idea to your team. Key individuals leave the meeting indicating disapproval of the idea. The disapproval is displayed verbally and non-verbally. The next team meeting is scheduled within five days. What can you do using reflection-on-action to reintroduce the idea for a holistic, authentic, and honest dialogue that includes all members of the team?

The importance of dialogue cannot be understated. The complexity of feelings, emotions, and cognition are exacerbated when dialogue is absent from reflective practice. Hilden and Tikkamäki (2013) explain that open dialogue as a form of collaborative reflection and inquiry aimed at exposing the meaning constructions based on which others think and act, thus creating shared understanding. It also aims at the collective question of assumptions, development of common language, and shared world view. The essential element is to instill rationales and attitudes that encourage change without creating blame or establishing failure as a common denominator. Sounding board or recap sessions that are action-oriented serve as a powerful tool to improve clarification. Engaging all team members in the process can also enhance development and understanding of key performance indicators, thus producing baseline questions for reflection-on-action and reflection-for-action considerations and results. Likewise, creating storyboards that display past, present, and future actions can aid in critical reflection and transformational learning.

This process of collaborative reflection invites team members to communicate experiences and share stories exploring current practices and informed next steps for teams and organizations. Relevance is a driving force. Remaining relevant with stakeholders requires engagement with current and potentially future perspectives. Individuals, teams, and organizations must consider how past and present can influence future opportunities. One element that cannot be overlooked within the reflective process is motivation. According to Wlodkowski (2008), motivation is important not only because it apparently improves learning but also because it is a consequence of learning.

Effort is a primary indicator of motivation. Individuals and teams engage with one another consistently and with intensity when motivated, compared to non-motivated participants. Reflective participants who are motivated can elevate the entire process when a caring atmosphere and environment prioritizing concentration are present, allowing both a sense of effort and spirit of cooperation to flourish. Wlodkowski (2008) also notes that sometimes one of the best ways to encourage adults to reconsider their position is to reflect back what they say so that they understand the impact of their words or can begin to identify their underlying assumptions.

Case Study

Team A is assigned a project that requires review of a process improvement to the company's recruitment of qualified applicants for their Research and Development Department. Community stakeholders are complaining about the difficulty the company has in the recruitment and employment of qualified women and candidates of color from local colleges.

Maria is assigned to lead a team of nine colleagues employed with strategic departments interfacing with research and development from across the organization. The company CEO addressed the team with parameters outlining the assignment, insisting the team not be constrained by existing human resources and company policy.

Maria embraces practice as a practitioner and leader. She wants to engage the process as a transformational learning effort encouraging team members to share their experience with the hiring process. During the process, some team members introduced the concept of inviting community members, local college career specialists, and diversity/equity professionals to share their insights regarding the company's hiring process. Reactions to the concept are mixed with some team members becoming emotional and storming out of the meeting.

Maria adjourns the meeting and is perplexed on next steps about how best to move forward with healing activities for the team.

The team is in the initial stages of the process. Using reflective practice,

1. What steps must Maria engage to reconvene the team?
2. Outline how transformational learning and experience are a part of the process to move forward.
3. What variables support or diminish the reflective process within the team?
4. How can Maria use the concept of community and shared experiences to strengthen each step she takes within the reflective process?

Conclusion

Mindfulness is a supporting feature of reflective practice. Practitioners can use mindfulness as a support for professional development to encourage the process of self and team awareness to manage stressors during projects and group interactions designed to accomplish goals. Examining who we are, questioning our views of the work, and understanding our place within projects are important steps leading to mindfulness. Being in touch while cultivating an appreciation for team members and their suggestions leads to moments in which we are fully engaged within reflective practice.

Thinking and acting proactively within reflective practice brings practitioners to encourage non-judgmental reactions of what is present during the inactions within teams. The objective is to engage mindfulness by paying attention to members' experiences, thoughts, and emotions. With reflective practice, team members are encouraged to be in the moment without pushing away from team members. Kabat-Zinn (2003) suggests that mindfulness encourages us to be present to whatever our experience is at that moment. It can broadly be understood in terms of practice that is available to anyone for encouraging the development of qualities, such as awareness, insight, and compassion. In Chapter 5, we will explore mindfulness as a tool that encourages practitioners to be present while also embracing experiences within the process of reflective practice. Mindfulness aids professional and personal development, helping deepen our appreciation and interactions.

References

Boud, D., Keogh, D., & Walker, D. (1985). *Reflection: Turning experience into learning.* New York: Routledge.

Healey, M. L., & Grossman, M. (2018, June 25). Cognitive and affective perspective-taking: Evidence for shared and dissociable anatomical substrates. *Frontiers in Neurology, 9,* 491. doi:10.3389/fneur.2018.00491. Retrieved from https://www.ncbi.nlm.nih.gov/pmc/articles/PMC6026651/

Hilden, S., & Tikkamäki, K. (2013). Reflective practice as a fuel for organizational learning. *Administrative Sciences, 3*(3):76–95. Retrieved from https://www.mdpi.com/2076-3387/3/3/76

Kabat-Zinn, J. (2003). Mindfulness-based interventions in context: Past, present and future. *Clinical Psychology: Science and Practice, 10,* 144–156.

McGoff, C. (2011). *The primes: how any group can solve any problem?* New York: Victory Publishers.

Mezirow, J. (2000). *Learning as transformation: Critical perspectives on a theory in progress.* San Francisco, CA: Jossey-Bass.

Qutoshi, B. S. (2018). Critical reflective practice as an approach to developing transformative learning-theory. *Dhaulagiri Journal of Sociology and Anthropology, 12,* 107–111.

Sherwood, D. G., & Horton-Deutsch, S. (2015). *Reflective organizations: On the frontlines of QSEN & reflective practice implementation.* Indianapolis, IN: Sigma Theta Tau International.

Sze Goh, A. Y. (2019). Rethinking reflective practice in professional learning using learning metaphors. *Studies in Continuing Education, 4*(1), 1–16. doi:10.1080/0158037X.2018.1474867.

Thy Jensen, U., & Ladegaard Bro, L. (2018). How transformational leadership supports intrinsic motivation and public service motivation: The mediating role of basic need satisfaction. *American Review of Public Administration, 48*(6), 535–549.

Volpe-White, M. J., Guthrie, L. K., & Torres, M. (2019). *Thinking to transform: Reflection in leadership learning.* Charlotte, NC: Information Age Publishing.

Wlodkowski, J. R. (2008). *Enhancing adult motivation to learn: A comprehensive guide for teaching all adults.* San Francisco, CA: John Wiley and Sons.

5
REFLECTION AS MINDFULNESS

Reflection Is Interwoven

As we move from reflective practice in a theoretical sense and develop into active participants in our own learning, reflection becomes a vital component to our professional development. Mindfulness at its best can help individuals during each stage of reflective practice by helping the navigation of difficult thoughts and emotions without becoming overwhelmed or shutting down emotionally. By encouraging pausing and observing, the mind may help people reset from being stuck in their story and as a result may empower them to move forward.

One definition of mindfulness is "… the act of remaining in the moment in order to respond authentically and nonjudgmentally to situations that arise" (Owens & Daul-Elhindi, 2020, p. 13). Mindfulness is about being fully aware of whatever is happening in the present moment without filters or lens of judgment or reaction. It can be brought to professional, casual, and family situations. Simply stated, mindfulness consists of building awareness of the mind and body and living in the here and now. The universal concept is learned behavior requiring individuals to notice and pay attention to thoughts and feelings of existing patterns of behavior that often result in stress that impacts relationships at work or at home. Mindfulness is observing, watching, and examining.

The actions of mindfulness are designed to move away from judging to allow individuals to become scientists of their minds. The science of mindfulness provides ample tools to help understanding and potentially change the unconscious responses of stress. Other benefits include improved thinking skills, faster reaction times, and less inclination toward various forms of stress.

The practice of mindfulness can improve the ability to proactively manage stress which allows people to build a tolerance for work-related challenges. This can also help improve people's critical thinking skills, as this is a skill that comes with practice. By engaging the present moment (reflection-in-action) without being judgmental, one can become proactive in the here and now, which increases engagement among team members. With increased capacity for innovation and creativity, mindfulness allows team members to find new possibilities in difficult group or interpersonal relations by replacing habitual reactions with more considered responses.

> **MIRROR MOMENT**
>
> Robert H. Schuller is credited with posing this introspective question: "What would you attempt if you knew you could not fail?" Considering that prompt coupled with what you have read about reflection through mindfulness thus far, what would you like to accomplish if you had increased capability to manage stress, think creatively, and plan boldly? How would your decisions look in your life – personally and/or professionally?

Conversation, however, takes time. We need to sit together, listen, worry, and dream together. As this age of turmoil tears us apart, we need to reclaim time to be together. Otherwise, we cannot stop the fragmentation. And, we need to be able to talk with those we have named "enemy." Fear of each other also keeps us apart. Most of us have lists of people we fear – We can't imagine talking with them, and if we did, we assume it would only create more anger. We can't imagine what we would learn from them, or what might become possible if we spoke to those we most fear. Our hope is that we can reclaim conversation as our route back to each other, and as the path forward to a hopeful future. It only requires imagination and courage and faith. These are qualities processed by everyone, to some extent or another, and now is the time to exercise them to their fullest (Wheatley, 2002).

Research indicates that mindfulness can help individuals process internal and external stimuli, feelings, and ideas from a neutral vantage point (Whitaker & Brannon, 2022). This non-judgmental angle dovetails with reflection as a focus within the learning experience, as well. Experiential learning theory, from Kolb and Kolb (2005) perspective, indicates that learning occurs through a blend of Concrete Experience and Abstract Conceptualization, coupled with Reflective Observation and Active Experimentation. The cyclical process of Kolb's theory takes a learner through the stages of experience, reflection, thinking, and acting.

Like the four tires of an automobile, Kolb's experiential stages carry the individual forward through new learning opportunities. However, reflective practice is more than just an individual component of the learning process; it should be interwoven throughout the experience. Rather than a single wheel, think of reflection as the tread on *all* of the tires. Tread keeps the vehicle grounded – quite literally, by providing traction with the street below. Likewise, reflection can anchor the entire learning experience through mindful practice.

Kolb's experiential learning theory provides a conceptual frame from which learners can strategize development and leadership within an organizational model, by using reflective practice as a foundation for growth. As mentioned above, the four "tires" of Kolb's theory are intended to drive us to deeper learning opportunities through experience and reflective practice. The use of each phase in Kolb's cycle leads to foundational ways of approaching, analyzing, and solving a problem. Reflection serves as the air that keeps the tires inflated. Each component of reflective practice (reflection-on-action, reflection-in-action, and reflection-for-action) are key pieces within Kolb's theory.

Within educational and business organizations, individuals share collective and concurrent experiences working with colleagues during formal and informal situations. Each situation is the beginning of the experiential learning process. Collective memory is formed and referred to as a part of a building block process of individual and/or shared experiences. Reflective practice aids learners with the ability to analyze and choose appropriate modes of behavior and problem solving tactics to convey the experiences into flexible and discerning approaches to organizational concerns and problems.

Experiential learning theory, reflective practice, and mindfulness can be described as a mind–body interaction. Each applied in a collective approach to learning, team and individual development, demonstrates a unified body of work and knowledge that leads to organizational improvements. The improvements can lead to health, wellbeing, and the cultural growth of a group and/or learner. It is important to acknowledge the small and large discussions within an organization to discover the trends embedded within experience, reflection, and mindful consideration.

Incorporating the goal of equity within facilitation of discourse provides exceptional opportunity for cultural development leading toward the examination of shared beliefs, values, and policies. The goal is to turn inward to begin honest, open, truthful conversation using the tools and concepts provided within reflective practice, experiential learning, and mindfulness to explore self-awareness. Additionally, we want to explore power structures built on assumptions to strengthen self-awareness by acknowledging areas we can better understand and address the difficulties to benefit change within teams and organizations.

> **MIRROR MOMENT**
>
> Mindfulness can be described as "focus, clarity, creativity, and compassion in the service of others" (Marturano, 2014, p. 11). What changes might you notice within your team – at work, school, or within your community – if everyone exhibited those traits? Consider immediate changes, as well as short-term and long-term improvements.

Like reflection in-action, mindfulness represents an open awareness and/or attention to inner experience and actions. Mindfulness must be unbiased in its awareness and actions, while individual and group bias can be unveiled within reflection-in-action. Mindfulness requires an unbiased awareness of openness and attention to inner experience. According to Brown, Ryan, and Creswell (2007), rather than generating mental accounts about the self, mindfulness offers a bare display of what is taking place. With this observant stance comes the possibility for unbiased information processing and consequently greater opportunities for adaptive self-regulation and wellbeing for individuals and teams.

Associations between mindfulness and reflective practice can be illustrated as a primary form of self-regulation (self-control) that must be utilized by practitioners. Both of these practices are likely a product of successful self-regulation. Regulation of the self is a key element in allowing individuals and teams the opportunity to collect information, data, and input from others before providing opinions and reactions. Mindfulness as an instrument within reflective practice raises the possibility of interventions that can represent instances of self-control exercise, and it is the resulting enhancement in self-control that helps explain the positive effects of interventions with reflective practice (Brown et al., 2007).

Typical of educational, governmental, and business cultures is a tendency to avoid talking about fear, difficulties, and stress. It's almost as if mental and emotional difficulties are a no-go-zone, which is ironic, since people universally face these and other challenges daily. Mindfulness helps us recognize that the choice to react to stimuli in our environment is entirely up to us. It supports our ability to calmly consider opposing views, but in no way prevents us from speaking up when we recognize flaws, fallacies, or injustice in messages, arguments, or events around us (Velott & Forte, 2019). The benefits to individual and team performance support the tools required in reflective practice. Benefits impact an improved performance according to an organization, including

- Better communication with team
- More effective people management skills

- Dealing with conflict more effectively
- Improved work life balance
- Increased innovation
- Individuals being better able to focus
- Being more productive

According to Kings and Wardropper (2016), a culture committed to supporting mindfulness must consider organic growth. The implementation must center on evolution and not revolution. Mindfulness can grow organically and slowly through word of mouth and observation of benefits. It can also grow through colleagues' experiences gaining the methods and arts of practice through interactions and becoming mindful advocates within reflective practice.

An aspect of reflective practice and mindfulness that becomes intriguing is the journey of embracing an approach of equanimity. This process allows current difficulties to be acknowledged and gives practitioners the freedom to

- Respectfully start challenging projects more easily
- Catch unhelpful thoughts which focus only on skills gaps
- Relate more readily to colleagues with different priorities in the implementation of strategy

Reflective practice like mindfulness takes practice, it is not accomplished in a single training or reading a book. Mindfulness and reflective practice consists of intention, attention, and attitude.

Embracing these three elements assists practitioners in becoming successful in developing and maintaining the connections integrated within reflective practice and mindfulness. The intent is initially one of self-control and beneficence. Tisdell and Riley (2019) elaborate, as practice progresses, one's intent can shift to self-exploration and finally toward liberation from automatic reaction. As with reflective practice, one of the primary goals of mindfulness is to focus on the nature of direct experience both internal and external and on minimizing the impact of interpretation. If practiced regularly and with the appropriate intention and attitude, mindfulness has shown to help practitioners reduce stress, increase compassion, and foster a more positive attitude.

Theoretical/Cultural Background of Mindfulness

Mindfulness – as a philosophical practice – stems from deeply rooted Eastern spiritual traditions, most notably, Buddhism (Shonin, Van Gordon, & Griffiths, 2014). Over time, certain secular techniques focused on physical and mental health – particularly treatments geared toward issues such as addiction and stress management – began adapting mindfulness practices, as well (Jones Medine, 2021).

Researchers have intertwined the notion of mindfulness with that of creativity (Carson & Langer, 2006). Mindfulness is not centered around arrival at a central place or about repairing anything. However, it is an encouragement to permit one to embrace where we already are and to learn the internal and external terrain of direct experience encountered in the space and time of an activity. This provides an awareness of a total gamut of our interactive experiences for past and present moments.

As individuals and teams deploy the concepts of mindfulness, within reflective practice, we discover that practitioners can distort planning and development sessions through editing and distortion by routinized, habitual, and unexamined activity of our thoughts and emotions, often involving significant alienation from direct experience of the sensory world that Buddhism encourages its followers to embrace. Mindfulness – in its capacity to more clearly and fully inform on what is taking place – may act as an integrative agent by enhancing capacities to act congruently with one's perceptions, reflectivity, considered goals, and self-endorsed values (Brown et al., 2007).

> **MIRROR MOMENT**
>
> Carolyn M. Jones Medine, a scholar of religion and culture, referred to mindfulness as a "call to conscience of practice," particularly with regard to intercultural exchanges (2021). Considering your own organization or institution, how does mindfulness play a role in Diversity, Equity, and Inclusion work (if at all)? How might you adapt reflective practice and mindfulness within your sphere of influence at your school or workplace?

Mindfulness Is Creativity

Mindfulness is typically defined in terms of awareness of one's surroundings, such as "... the ability to be fully present, and aware of where we are and what we are doing, without becoming overly reactive or overwhelmed by the present. Mindfulness is often associated with meditation practices, aimed at building skills for present-moment awareness as a mental habit ..." (Henriksen, Richardson, & Shack, 2020, p. 2).

Mindfulness encourages one to take a moment in time to wonder, think before passing judgment. It is an important part of the transformational theory that underlines reflective practice. It is about waking up and witnessing what is present and offered in the moment. Challenging because of the urgency to discuss concepts often overrules the ability to engage transitional tools that permit moving to reflection-on-action, reflective-in-action, and reflective-for-action. The goal is to engage transformational learning as a foundational theory to support reflective practice. This is essential to unlocking the mindfulness process that encourages an examination of our values, goals, and processes designed to generate beliefs and opinions that are proven to be authentic, true, inclusive, open, and whole.

Creating concepts for review that are capable of change and justified to guide individual and group actions that guide our work, this approach is referred to as change that is meaningful and productive, addressing the mental connection of experience and reflection. Transformation permits and/or encourages a path toward change in one or more of an individuals or team's beliefs, attitudes, or goals. Reflective practice aids the awakening of moving away from beliefs, attitudes, and goals that are taken for granted, to a process of reexamination of definitions and the creation of shared frameworks that invite meaningful change.

Davis (2014) noted that most individual and team organizations, when confronted with poor performance or unsatisfactory results, begin to formulate excuses, rationalizations, and arguments for why they should not be held accountable or at least, not fully accountable for an organization's problems. Such cultures of failed accountability or victimization have weakened business character, stressing ease over difficulty, feeling good over being good, appearance over substance, saving face over solving problems, and illusion over reality. Through transformational learning we are freed from uncritical acceptance of others' purposes, values, beliefs, and actions.

Transformations in the habits of groups, individuals, and teams using reflective practice can be sudden and dramatic (reflection-in-action), slower (reflection-on-action), or incremental (reflection-for-action), leading to change in business, individual and team processes.

Wheatley (2002) suggests the practice of conversation takes courage, faith, and time. We don't get it right the first time, and we don't have to. We settle into conversation; we don't just do it. As we risk talking to each other about something we care about, we become curious about each other; as we slow things down, gradually we remember this timeless way of being together. Our rushed and thoughtless behaviors fade away and we sit quietly in the gift of being together.

Mindfulness in the Real World

Unlike self-control, mindfulness is not primarily a tool to keep the self-moving in a preordained direction. It is rather the capacity to, first and foremost, be aware of the ongoing parade put on by the self, including one's attempts to exert self-control. Indeed mindfulness may even permit better choices about whether and when to control the self in the service of chosen ends, and when it might be better to step out of the parade. There is general agreement that mindfulness concerns an unbiased open observation of all of one's experience, mental somatic and sensorial. Mindfulness is pertinent to all aspects of experience and may have important consequences that extend beyond mindful attention to thought (Brown et al., 2007).

1. Learning is more of a process than a checklist of outcomes.
2. New ideas build upon previously understood ideas.
3. Conflict resolution steers the process of learning.
4. Learning is not just about gaining knowledge – rather, it involves the whole person.
5. Learning involves a blend of a person and their environment.
6. Learning builds upon itself; it is not simply a dissemination of knowledge.

Tisdell and Riley (2019) state that often the intention behind mindfulness is initially one of self-control. As practice progresses one's intent can shift to self-exploration and liberation from automatic reactions. Qualities of mindfulness are steps, concepts, and actions focused on direct experience and the minimization of the interpretation. Experiential learning as a component of mindfulness allows for review of situations based on prior engagement, always being sensitive to differences in individual and team needs, including contextual factors that might have an impact on how others might perceive various activities. The evaluation of mindfulness and experiential learning within reflective practice can assist teams in remaining above the line of accountability.

People and organizations find themselves thinking and behaving below the line of accountability whenever they consciously or unconsciously avoid accountability for individual or collective results. The deployment of reflective practice can assist individuals and team members avoiding the victim cycle/blame game and move toward residing above the line of accountability. Outlining the experiences and actions that led to a dysfunctional system/culture of service is often the primary step. Experiential learning leads to mindful conversations and sharing of positive and negative concepts and emotions that are often not shared between team members. The direct embodiment of experience through collaborative input with others can lead to cultural change, improved practices, values, beliefs, and a redesigned organizational mission and vision.

Reflective Practice in the Workplace

Reflection and informed action comprise important details of leadership development. Importantly, there is a need for training allowing reflective practice of mindfulness to be used as a tool (Davis, 2014). Mindfulness in leadership, or slowing down and attending to the present moment, promises to prompt rational decision making and effective organizational practices for both leaders and followers.

Mindfulness can improve morale and subsequently decrease employee turnover. This cultivation fosters empathy for others. The empathy derived from mindfulness places leaders and learners in a space that illuminates their connections to the workplace community. According to Davis (2014), reflection and informed action comprise key elements of leadership development and application within the workplace. Specifically, a need exists for administrative training to entail the reflective practice of mindfulness and its impact on training both the hearts and minds of leaders and learners. Practices that include a single pointed concentration, silence, and quieting or clearing the mind, and the creative process of journaling are mindful contemplative practices useful for a leadership curriculum. Other practices are the generative practice of social justice issues and the relational practice of dialogue, deep listening, council circles, and storytelling.

Action Research in Daily, Reflective Practice

Action research has successfully been used to facilitate change and improve service in industry, education, community development, and public sector engagements. Action research can be described as collaborative because it involves practitioners in the actual process of research, as opposed to the practitioners being researched. The process of action research provided a forum for constructing a bridge between theory and practice and while enabling the participants to reflect. It provides a cohesive extension to reflective practice. Carr and Kemmis (1986) outline action research to include the following elements:

- Focusing on change and improvement
- Involving practitioners in the research process
- Being educational for those involved
- Looking at questions that arise from practice
- Being a cyclical process of collecting, feeding back, and reflecting on data
- Being a process which generates knowledge

The action research process engages participants sharing/working together within groups, creating a plan for the actual research, the plan is then actualize with a given setting, once the plan is actualized results (data) are gathered reviewed and reflection occurs, once there is conscientious, action plans (steps) are developed and implemented, data are again collected for review and reflection, and the final step is to create change based on results. Action research is cyclical; therefore, the process begins again with the *plan* phase (Figure 5.1).

Action Research Process

From adult learning theory, successful learning is most likely to occur when learning is based in the real world of the learners; when they have a sense of responsibility for what they learn; when learning is problem based; and

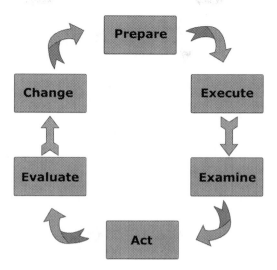

FIGURE 5.1 Action research process

when learning is active, experiential, and driven by inquiry (Rodgers, 1969). Faculty and leaders have a responsibility to practitioners in which activities such as action research are used to highlight the importance of critical reflections on individual and group practices (Huang, 2010).

Action researchers do not readily separate understanding and action, rather they argue that only through action is legitimate understanding possible: Theory without practice is not theory but speculation. The major element to action research is the practitioners; they are partners in the development of knowledge creation. This creation comes from experience and requires a reflective process to be effective. Each phase of reflective practice can stimulate practitioners and leaders in a thoughtful transformative process toward improvement and change.

The nucleus of action research is that the work or engagement occurs within a state of action. It is important that one gets into an environment and engages with practitioners within the organization. Action research performs best in association with practitioners and requires communication with the participants to share and shape research questions and design. Practitioners must be willing to engage in the experiment. Researchers plan for cycles of action, reflection, and therefore, must be reflective by examining how activities occur, and the possible impact an intervention might encounter. Following is an example of action research, using a college readmission policy as a scenario:

> Back Drop: The Dean of Arts and Sciences develops standards and policy for students seeking readmission to the college after a two-semester absence.

Objective: The goal of the readmission study is to help potential readmit students receive the academic support and professional guidance required from faculty, staff, and on campus service providers for degree completion within two years of readmission to the college.

Research Practice: A group of faculty, support staff, deans, and students was convened. They were asked to identify potential academic and student services existing policies that inhibited readmission and successful program completion, they wished to address with new policy and procedures. The group then met for a workshop with dialogue and review of current policy that served as barriers to readmission.

Common Action: A cross-functional planning work platform was provided to assist in capturing new ideas. A format was designed for developing each idea into an actionable planning decision. With the support of the Dean of Arts and Sciences the actionable items and supporting data were packaged into a new college plan for readmission. The group presented the package of policies to the College President and Leadership Team.

Outcomes: The new policies were adopted by the leadership team. The intervention planning produced improvements in the readmission process. It also provided insights on why students discontinue enrollment. Also, insights were provided into the financial difficulty that impedes readmission. It also provided feedback from currently enrolled students to lessen the gap between administrators, faculty, policymakers, and students by developing sustainable cycles of improvement for dialogue and feedback for and with community stakeholders.

Case Study

Action research represents a variety of methods that are used in research and problem solving within communities and organizations. As a research approach, it can be categorized as an extension to reflective practice. Action research has several characteristics:

1. It is practical in terms of dealing with real-life issues.
2. It is focused on generating change in practices.
3. It is a cyclical process whereby critical reflection on practice leads to research findings that can generate possibilities for change.
4. It is participative with participants being active in the research process.

Use the four characteristics to design an action research activity with your colleagues to examine the resources available in your local community for residents to access public transit. Share your design and planned research activities with your colleagues.

Conclusion

In any situation, one must be sensitive to differences in practitioners' needs and how they process contextual information that can impact how they perceive activities and engagements that are mindful. Despite all the requests for knowledge development within our society, there is often a lack of dissemination of educational knowledge shared between sectors of business, educational institutions, and community-based agencies. The use of action research to guide development and evaluate knowledge for planning and development of goals, values, and outcomes has the ability to lead to inclusive engagement by using cross-functional change management approaches.

Reflective practice and mindfulness are interconnected and supported by action research. Action research engages reflection as a perspective of the process of change. Through mindfulness, variables such as context and collaboration with others, and change over time can be incorporated into the perspectives of process improvement with community stakeholders joining research projects that engage trend analysis, data review, and dialogue that seeks an end result inclusive of new beginnings.

References

Brown, K. W., Ryan, R. M., & Creswell, J. D. (2007). Addressing fundamental questions about mindfulness. *Psychological Inquiry*, 18(4), 272–281.

Carr, W., & Kemmis, S. (1986). *Becoming critical: Education, knowledge and action research*. London, England: Falmer Press.

Carson, S. H., & Langer, E. J. (2006). Mindfulness and self-acceptance. *Journal of Rational-Emotive and Cognitive-Behavior Therapy*, 24, 29–43. doi:10.1007/s10942-006-0022-5.

Davis, J. D. (2014). Mindfulness in higher education: Teaching, earning, and leadership. *The International Journal of Religion and Spirituality in Society*, 4(3), 1–5.

Henriksen, D., Richardson, C., & Shack, K. (2020). Mindfulness and creativity: Implications for thinking and learning. *Thinking Skills and Creativity*, 37, 100689. doi:10.1016/j.tsc.2020.100689.

Huang, H. (2010). What is good action research? *Action Research*, 8, 93–109.

Jones Medine, C. M. (2021). Natal and convert Buddhism and mindfulness. *Buddhist-Christian Studies*, 41, 33–58.

Kings, R., & Wardropper, E. (2016). Creating mindful culture within financial services, capital one. In M. Chapman-Clarke (Ed.), *Mindfulness in the workplace: An evidence-based approach to improving wellbeing and maximizing performance*. London, England: Kogan Page, 96.

Kolb, A. Y., & Kolb, D. A. (2005). learning styles and learning spaces: Enhancing experiential learning in higher education. *Academy of Management Learning & Education*, 4(2), 193–212.

Marturano, J. (2014). *Finding the space to lead: A practical guide to mindful leadership*. New York: Bloomsbury Press.

Owens, T. M., & Daul-Elhindi, C. A. (2020). *The 360 Librarian: A framework for integrating mindfulness, emotional intelligence, and critical reflection in the workplace,*

Association of College & Research Libraries. *ProQuest Ebook Central*. Retrieved from https://ebookcentral-proquest-com.ezproxy.fhsu.edu/lib/fhsu/detail.action?docID=6006608

Rodgers, C. R. (1969). *Freedom to learn*. Columbus, OH: Charles Merrill Publication.

Shonin, E., Van Gordon, W., & Griffiths, M. D. (2014). The emerging role of Buddhism in clinical psychology: Toward effective integration. *Psychology of Religion and Spirituality*, 6(2), 123–137. doi:10.1037/a0035859.

Tisdell, J. E., & Riley, T. D. (2019). The landscape of mindfulness and meditation in adult education: A partial prescription (and critique) for lifelong learning and well-being. *New Directions for Adult and Continuing Education*, 2019(161), 9–20.

Velott, D., & Forte, S. K. (2019). Toward health equity: Mindfulness and cultural humility as adult education. *New Directions for Adult and Continuing Education*, 161, 57–66.

Wheatley, J. M. (2002). *Turning to one another, simple conversation to restore hope to the future*. San Francisco, CA: Berrett-Koehler Publishers.

Whitaker, W. K., & Brannon, L. A. (2022). Mindfulness and implementation planning: Promoting self-reported and behavioral forgiveness. *Psychological Reports*, 1–22. doi:10.1177/00332941221100450.

6
REFLECTION AS PERSPECTIVE

Author and speaker John Maxwell (2012) is credited with bringing this question into the mainstream of leadership and management discussions: "Are you really leading, or are you just taking a walk?" A person in a supervisory position – the boss, manager, president, or CEO – is a de facto leader, by nature of their job description. As we will dig into more deeply in this chapter, however, not all managers are good leaders, and some individuals in non-managerial roles can be excellent leaders. We will explore some of the history and shift in mindset from management to leadership, then turn our attention to what it means to lead through change as we continue on our journeys to become more reflective administrators.

The Evolution from Management to Leadership

In the early 1970s, forward-thinking technology scholars George Kozmetsky and Timothy Ruefli predicted that the field of management would gain legitimacy in future years because of the way leaders would be able to understand their roles through social, economic, and cultural perspectives, with the ability to "… predict the consequences of their actions with greater certainty than is possible today" (1971, p. 18). Like the foundational days of the strictly hierarchical American bureaucracy that we discussed in Chapter 1 were to the public sector, management within the private sector used to be understood as efficiency of operations and technical competency. From both vantage points, employees were entities to be trained, supervised, and evaluated, not necessarily encouraged to pursue their own professional development or supported to make changes in their career paths.

A common example of this traditional management mindset is the quintessential retirement watch, which hearkens back to the time of the "Great Generation" (pertaining to those who came of age around the WWII era), yet the symbolism of such tokens to celebrate career longevity with an individual company was also passed down to the Baby Boomers. Just as the idea of merely management has evolved into a more comprehensive notion of leadership across both the private and public sectors, so, too, have the expectations of a young person pursuing a singular path for the entirety of their career become more lax over time to allow for flexibility along the career ladder (to include even climbing a completely new ladder by changing professions).

Another step in managerial evolution is the way many professions have moved beyond the assumption of "leader" as "boss." There is a recognition nowadays that leadership occurs *beyond* positions that have an institution or industry-wide responsibility such as senior leader or middle manager positions. There has been a shift in the leadership studies field that decenters leadership from the individual-only perspective when the manager is equated to leadership, to one that also embraces a more distributed, shared, and collaborative approach beyond these titled individuals.

A leadership-as-practice approach starts first with process, rather than the traits of individuals and a structuralist assumption informed by organizational role and work arrangements. This perspective stands in contrast from previous configurations that pre-established individual leaders based on their assigned roles. It is also important to move beyond focusing only on a managerial–collegial duality due to the numerous shifts in employee responsibilities institutions have undergone. Too often, the lines of demarcation used to define areas or divisions of responsibilities are blurred and cross-over departments.

Alternative models such as distributed leadership or shared leadership can appear to be a possible remedy to the divisions and tensions that permeate institutions. If leadership is positioned as a phenomenon akin to influence, while distribution is associated with sharing, then the focus becomes one of origin and yield: Which entity or individual wields influence, and how is the power dynamic balanced? If work labeled as *leadership* originates and is distributed by the few to the many, then distributed leadership becomes a functional tool of work activity and can continue to reinforce and protect existing power structures. However, if leadership focuses less on roles and more on encompassing origins from within the institution, tensions and problems that are within the organization have the opportunity to come to the surface rather than being buried.

Many leadership theories start with the assumption that leadership is wedded to the traits and behaviors of the individual, in other words, a leader-centric view of leadership. Coupled with this – and sometimes uncritically acknowledged – is the reliance on this assumption as the means to deliver and uphold reform. This perspective can disproportionately suit those in power to maintain the structures that favor a preferred way of viewing and promoting organizational practices. The argument here is not to do away with organizational goals or organizational roles where some roles have more authority than others; rather it is to bring to the surface sometimes unquestioned norms that can prevent alternative ways of understanding and learning about practice.

Developing Leader Pipelines

Empowering leadership is described as a leadership method demarcating performances for power-sharing with subordinates. It is a method of making a feasible environment to distribute the authority with workers. The practice often leads to power-sharing by engaging the experience and knowledge of workers. This practice also leads to valuing the contributions of workers and assigning decision-making autonomy and responsibility to informal leaders throughout the organization.

Institutional performance and development depend upon employees' efficiency and competence. Higher performance encourages strategic human resource techniques and expands strategic tactics of management, showing belief in workers' capabilities and giving them autonomy to act according to the condition. In service-oriented positions, employees adjust to conditions they encounter using organizational policies and practices. Their performance is considered an influential factor for higher growth potential. However, in competitive global economic conditions, all service organizations, including educational institutions, are emphasizing more on empowering employees and necessitating supportive behavior with subordinates.

Today, the practice of upholding archaic structures of directing and controlling employees is outmoded. It has been replaced by providing permission and authorization to employees to react and make decisions. Effective leaders give authority and are inclusive of decision-making and encouraging toward self-management. On the contrary, low empowering leaders offer limited chances for autonomy and discourage self-management. Empowered personnel have advanced capability to acquire a higher level of efficiency because they feel the wisdom of control and enhanced interdepartmental interaction within their job responsibilities. We will dig into empowerment further in Chapter 8, but the focus here is on leaders in any position making purposeful steps to empower those with whom they interact.

Empowering leadership is observed as an interpersonal link between leaders and employees. Specifically within higher education institutions, empowerment typically flows down from the top of the organization. The key to effective institutions of higher education follows a model that shares the governance across faculty and staff. This cooperation creates an empowering leadership format that leads to enhanced opportunities to identify potential leaders across the organization. It also leads to the review of various types/styles of leadership theory that use storytelling and appreciative inquiry along with leadership academies. This provides an important step to reimagining the organization and building a community of stakeholders that are important contributors to institutional mission, vision, goals, and beliefs.

Empowering leadership also establishes an understanding of ownership and autonomy that fosters vigilance among team members with attention toward departmental and organizational goals. This linkage model of leadership adapts goal clarity through maximizing psychological ownership and intrinsic motivation of partially self-determined goals. Goal clarity is the degree to which a supporter identifies accurately what targeted goals are and what they should achieve. With higher goal clarity, followers can identify assigned tasks as well as responsibilities, important objectives, and required expectations. Without goal clarity, staff can become unfocused and disinterested – thus engaging in extraneous activities that derail the focus on goals and allow the allocation of job responsibilities on tasks that do not actively contribute toward stakeholder service or performance.

Enhancing the meaningfulness of work, fostering participation in decision-making, expressing confidence in high performance, and providing autonomy from bureaucratic constraints are major elements of empowering leadership. It is believed that these specific leadership features would accelerate self-efficacy and enabling procedures of empowering leadership (self-efficacy can be identified as one's trust in their ability to be successful in a given circumstance, completing job related tasks).

Leading through Change

In a study on change leadership within the public sector, van der Voet (2016) found that top-down communication and active participation between affected parties were key elements to successful implementation of new initiatives. Interestingly, these two must-have components also overlap with the pillars of the Open Government Directive (2009), which was spearheaded by the Obama administration. The Open Government Directive was founded on three principles of transparency, participation, and collaboration, with an emphasis on building and protecting the public trust. To facilitate change effectively, leaders must respect each other's knowledge contributions and find new ways to identify and solve complex problems and challenges.

Transparency, as envisioned by the Open Government Directive, hinges on maintaining accountability through information shared publicly. In this way, the concept dovetails with van der Voet's call to action for managerial level communication. When all levels of an organization receive the same message from top leaders without sugar-coating or withholding information, it helps build trust. Participation, likewise, engages the public (or members of an organization) in a grassroots or bottom-up manner. Individuals and interest groups are able to share ideas and lend their expertise to help decision-makers understand the ramifications of policies and other changes under consideration.

While not explicitly covered in the van der Voet study, the third leg of the Open Government Directive bears mention here: Collaboration. If transparency is top-down and participation is primarily bottom-up, then collaboration is intertwined between layers of an organization or community. van der Voet did emphasize active participation, and a reflective administrator leading through periods of change must be willing to engage with internal and external partners, as well as across levels of the institution. Effective collaboration implemented through the Open Government Directive looks like an agency that utilizes technology to improve interactions with constituents, has an engaging forward-facing online presence, and makes use of innovative practices to connect with the general public, private sector, and non-profit agencies.

MIRROR MOMENT

In what ways have you experienced or observed collaboration done well at your institution or organization? How did the individuals and/or teams involved demonstrate both transparency and participation? What innovative practices, if any, did you notice?

Action Learning

Action learning is a means of development – intellectual, emotional, or physical – that requires its subject, through responsible involvement in some real, complex, and stressful problem, to achieve intended change sufficient to improve observable behavior henceforth in the problem field. In action learning, people learn with and from each other by mutual support, advice, and criticism during their engagement with real problems, intendedly to solve in whole or in part. Action learning represents a process of steps that requires reflection on an individual's work and beliefs in a supportive (sometimes confrontational) environment of peers for the purpose of gaining new insights and resolving real organizational problems in real time.

Running through all definitions of Action learning is a central theme of real problems that are the focus of learning for action. Another central theme is reflection as a means for learning. Each chapter in this text builds on the collaborative engagement required within reflective practice. Reflective practice is a way of making meaning out of what is happening (reflection-in-action), what has happened (reflection-on-action), and what can happen (reflection-for-action). This involves collaboration with colleagues in an effort to understand points of view, prior actions, and decision which is vitally important to action learning.

Fostering learning in the workplace and promoting a continuous learning process and reflection while providing support for colleagues with the intention of accomplishing tasks is central to the concept of Action Learning. The emphasis always is on getting things done, supporting reflection in order to reach new understandings and prompt changes in practice. This process of reflection and action is supported by peers in a learning set (Stocks, Trevitt, & Hughes, 2018).

Action Learning involves engagement at all levels of an organization is essential. Leaders and practitioners may not agree on a given course of action; however, engaging in problem-solving and action is a mandatory learning activity. Experiential learning is at the center of action learning. Learning is interpreted for past experiences, this represents the acquiring of new knowledge. The acquisition of new knowledge assists with the solving of new problems. New ideas generated by participants in an action learning process can spark additional ideas which can support the reflective practice process.

Action learning often occurs in learning sets composed of and supported by peers. The sets meet regularly over a predetermined period of time (weeks or months) for at least one hour or more. The sets provide a structure for convening in small numbers to address workplace concerns, ideas, and possible process improvements, or curriculum development. The members of a given set do not offer advice; however, they provide a confidential environment where members can examine their concerns openly (without fear of reprisal). Facilitators are present during the sets. The facilitator attends to planning and process, clock management, ensuring all members have the required space and opportunity to participate and contribute during each convening, along with helping each member of the work constructively on the concern being explored.

Action learning is learning by reflecting on what went well, what did not, and why, and learning from and with each other in small groups known as action sets. A structure for developing an action learning set includes the following:

- An invitation to participate. Practitioners are invited to join the set. Each is encouraged to identify and submit concerns/issues for exploration and discussion.
- Initial meeting. Collective decision-making on the issues/concerns to focus on within the set.
- Presentations. Team members whose concerns/issues was selected by the team, provides an overview and outline for questions and interpretation.

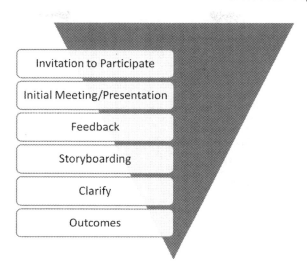

FIGURE 6.1 Action learning funnel

- Feedback. Each set member reveals their opinion and feeling after listening to each presentation.
- Appreciative/Storyboarding session is conducted to encourage set members to share images of their impressions in response to what they heard (develop a picture of the outcomes you imagine).
- Clarifying Questions after the appreciative inquiry/storyboarding session, time is provided for clarifying questions and answers.
- Outcomes:
  1. Reflection-in-action presenter leaves the immediate setting. The remaining members continue to explore and discuss the presentation and feedback (the presenter can listen to the discussions. However, they are not permitted to join the conversations).
  2. Reflection-on-action the presenter rejoins the set and shares their opinions regarding the discussions along with potential plans for moving forward.
  3. Reflection-for-action set members review and reflect on the process of action learning, and outcomes. The set members share and develop potential process improvements for future engagements (Figure 6.1).

What enables action learning to be powerful is its relative simplicity in practice, but relative complexity in the theories underlying action learning. Simply stated, action learning works so well because it has the unique ability to interweave a wide array of organizational, psychological, sociological, anthropological, educational, and political theories that form a foundation and synergy unavailable in any other source.

MIRROR MOMENT

What might effective collaboration look like within your agency or institution? With that ideal scenario in mind, consider obstacles that may hinder progress, whether they be personnel, procedural, or policy in nature. What parties would need to be engaged (both internally and external to the organization) to overcome those hurdles?

Destructive Leadership

Kahneman (2011) described risk factors within leadership this way: "Leaders who have been lucky are never punished for having taken too much risk. Instead, they are believed to have had the flair and foresight to anticipate success, and the sensible people who doubted them are seen in hindsight as mediocre, timid, and weak. A few lucky gambles can crown a reckless leader with a halo of prescience and boldness" (p. 204). Well-developed leadership agility skills to engage learners, employees, and external stakeholders are required if a leader hopes to guide current and future direction among the team and community.

The pace of change often seems to accelerate over time, and it is important for leaders to use skills, theories, practices, and experiential learning tools to advance opportunities and challenges to create the desired future. Leaders must invest in creative thought and innovative methods to determine what works and what does not work in the development and growth of the organization and its learners/employees. Change and challenge are the consistent concepts that drive the development of leadership. We looked at transformative learning in earlier chapters, but the concept is relevant again here because transformational, transitional, and passive-avoidant leadership are dimensions that can apply to leaders, as well as followers' perceptions of leaders' behaviors, attributes, and behaviors.

Zacher and Johnson (2015) note that transformational leadership involves the leader as a motivator to their employees by projecting as a positive role model, communicating, and projecting a proactive vision for the future, allowing independent and creative processing/input while displaying caring and developing opportunities for current/future nurturing for employee growth.6 Transformational leadership is considered to be the most effective form of leadership in the full range of leadership models, a claim that has been supported by numerous empirical studies.

Transactional leadership consists of the foundation of a fair and stable sharing of relationships between the leader and their charges by establishing a practice of detailing both the leaders' and charges' responsibilities and expectations, setting goals, and providing accommodations for completion of a job or task. Transactional leaders monitor work process, performance, and goal attainment before errors can occur. While transactional leadership is an effective form of leadership, it does not provide motivational engagement demonstrated within transformational leadership.

Passive-avoidant leadership is distinguished by the leader avoiding and neglecting important tasks, intervening only after mistakes are made, and avoiding proactive engagement with charges. The person responsible for leadership is passive, meaning that they are non-active and primarily out of touch with tasks, goals, and directives. Passive-avoidant leadership is considered a highly ineffective form of leadership behavior (or non-leadership, as the case may be). According to Zacher and Johnson (2015), transactional leadership is considered to be more effective than passive-avoidant leadership, but the transformational style is conceptualized as the most effective form of leadership in terms of followers' outcomes.

Challenging the Status Quo

Systemically adjusting a "That's the way we've always done it" mindset within an organization demands a commitment to change and a focus on adaptation. In order to determine the change directive, one must engage in reflection-on-action and reflection-for-action. Similar to transformational leadership, adaptive leadership is development centered. It is the practice of mobilizing people to tackle tough challenges and still thrive. The concept of thriving is drawn from evolutionary biology, in which a successful adaptation has three characteristics (Heifetz, Grashow, & Linskey, 2009):

1. Preserves the DNA essential for the species' continued survival
2. Discards (reregulates or rearranges) the DNA that no longer serves the species' current needs
3. Gives the species the ability to flourish in new ways and in more challenging environments. A living system develops that will make the best out of its history, well into the future

Organizational systems are not all that different from organic ones, as a matter of fact: successful adaptation at an institutional level also enables a system to thrive as a living organism (at least one comprised of such), as reflective administrators implement the best takeaways from their experiential learning history and mold them into current activities, future development, and attainment of the overarching mission, vision, and strategic plan. According to Heifetz et al. (2009), mobilizing people to meet their immediate adaptive challenges lies at the heart of leadership in the short term. Over time, these and other culture-shaping efforts build an organization's adaptive capacity, fostering processes that generate new norms that enable an organization to meet the ongoing stream of adaptive challenges posed by a world ever ready to offer new realities, opportunities, and pressures.

Heifetz et al. (2009) explain how successful adaptations enable a living system to take the best from its history into the future:

- Adaptive leadership is specifically about change that enables the capacity to thrive.
- Successful adaptive changes build on the past rather than jettisoning it (experiential learning theory).
- Organizational adaptation occurs through experimentation.
- Adaptation relies on diversity.
- New adaptations significantly displace, regenerate, and rearrange some old organizational DNA.
- Adaptation takes time (pp. 14–16).

Adaptive leaders not only embrace change for individual growth, but they also facilitate positive change within their organizations. Adaptive leadership behaviors can assist personnel and other stakeholders to address challenges using reflective practice to create necessary change to move the agency or institution forward. The adaptive leadership framework addresses the following three challenges (Heifetz, 1994):

1. Technical challenges
2. Technical and adaptive challenges that are clearly defined but require people beyond the leader to solve
3. Adaptive challenges not clearly defined, requiring individuals and teams beyond the leader to engage in solutions

In Chapter 2, we discussed professional competency as it pertains to technical expertise (hard skills such as software proficiency or financial acumen), coupled with soft skills like communication, cultural sensitivity, and conflict resolution. In this context, we are considering technical challenges at an organizational level, but the overlap is comparable. A technical challenge, for example, could be a university that acquires a new student information system or curriculum management package: executive leadership would negotiate the financial terms and deliverables of the contract.

The second category of technical *and* adaptive challenges at an institutional or organizational level could also be applied to the example above, when it comes to personnel and students needing to gain the technical skills to learn how to use the new software or cloud-based service. This combination challenge requires others besides the apparent leader to become involved in problem-solving the situation. In our scenario above, the executive leadership team at the college will need to delegate training to other professionals across campus to implement through workshops, self-help resources online, and other venues.

Lastly, a wholly adaptive challenge requires agile and creative problem-solving, because these are unanticipated problems that arise without warning or preparation. Leaders must put their reflection-in-action skills to use in order to tackle an adaptive challenge. Keeping with the new student information system adoption example, an adaptive challenge might bubble to the surface when contracts for Graduate Teaching Assistants (GTAs) processed incorrectly, because the system automatically assigned them to an hourly student employee category, rather than a salaried stipend. Human Resources, Information Technology, and the Graduate School must put their heads together to find a workaround promptly so that the GTAs can be paid on time. An adaptive challenge involves individuals and units outside of the executive leadership team working together to develop a solution.

> **MIRROR MOMENT**
>
> Without taking much time to dwell on your response, jot down the first five traits or qualities that describe your organization (workplace, school, etc.). Do these characteristics positively reflect how you would like the organization to be perceived? What would it look like to challenge the status quo? What types of processes, policies, and perspectives would need to evolve?

As with reflective practice, the process of adaptive leadership requires disciplined action, a review of experiential learning, and a focus on addressing problems. A critical step is always transferring ownership of the work back to the learners/employees. This happens when leaders take a step back and empower the individuals on their teams. In order for this to occur, the leader must protect from a rear position; they must take a backseat and let the team members drive. This action permits marginalized individuals to use their voice and feel they are being heard. Adaptive leadership is learner/employee centered. It encourages everyone to engage by incorporating reflective practice to interact, listen, and share while working toward solutions.

Case Study

A cultural climate study was recently conducted at a state land grant university, which invited feedback from students, faculty and staff, alumni, and the external community. The university president convened a campus-wide steering committee of leaders to review, discuss, and analyze the results. Survey participants were overwhelmingly in favor of change within the organization and its relationship with employees and community stakeholders. The mission and vision of the institution were deemed to be out of date and out of touch with student and community goals, aspirations, and development.

The survey revealed several trouble spots, which aligned with other worrisome trends like a declining student population over the past three years. In the anonymous comment portion of the survey, several employees frankly admitted their desire to seek employment elsewhere. Prominent community stakeholders and donors also questioned the future direction of the institution and its commitment to the community it serves. In addition, the survey findings suggested a lack of opportunities for the development of employees to assume leadership roles. It was determined that leadership was at the heart of the problem.

As one of the largest universities in the state, the institution has a complex organizational chart with multiple layers of management. During the steering committee meeting, a number of senior leaders attempted to deny the findings, asserting that more opportunities for leadership development existed than the survey findings suggested. Others in the committee, including certain members of the executive leadership team, admitted their lack of knowledge about what types of professional development initiatives were actually in place across campus.

Change appears to be central to the future of this university. Using what you have learned from this chapter, determine how you would design, develop, and support the development of a future leadership pipeline for the institution? Identify and explain the types of leadership necessary to help your plan come to fruition.

Conclusion

Communication is the most essential ingredient within reflective practice. It is used to identify group/team perspectives of experience. Our reflections are embedded in the skill of communication. "To begin with, the words people utter refer to common experience. They express facts, ideas or events that are communicable because they refer to a stock of knowledge about the world that other people share. Words also reflect their authors' attitudes and beliefs, their point of view, that are also those of others" (Kramsch, 2000, p. 3). Practitioners and leaders move from through the reflective prism of perspective to doubt within the context of language.

As a community, reflective practitioners create experience through language. This occurs through various communication methods while engaging with individuals, groups, or teams, for example, person to person, technology (emails and text messages), writing, and telephone. The means used to communicate establishes common meanings that are understood by the team they belong to. Communication plays a major role in establishing and/or changing our view of an employment or family situation. It can also alter our worldview, which we will address in more detail in Chapter 7. However, these restrictive doubts can be explored and reimagined through reflective practice. Through critical reflection, individuals, groups, and teams can explore new insights and methods to embrace challenges in approaches that establish foundations of information and knowledge based on theory (existing or new) and the development of new and exciting fields of professional practice (Matthews, 2020).

References

Heifetz, R. A. (1994). *Leadership without easy answers* (Vol. 465). Cambridge, MA: Harvard University Press.

Heifetz, R. A., Grashow, A., & Linsky, M. (2009). *The practice of adaptive leadership: Tools and tactics for changing your organization and the world*. Boston, MA: Harvard Business Press.

Kahneman, D. (2011). *Thinking, fast and slow*. New York: Farrar, Straus and Giroux, p. 204.

Kozmetsky, G., & Ruefli, T. (1971). *Information technology and its impacts*, as quoted in G. Kozmetsky & P. Yue, *Economic transformation of the United States, 1950-2000*, Purdue University Press. (2004). *ProQuest Ebook Central*, p. 18. Retrieved from https://ebookcentral-proquest-com.ezproxy.fhsu.edu/lib/fhsu/detail.action?docID=3398615

Kramsch, C. (2000). *Language and culture*. Oxford, England: Oxford University Press.

Matthews, J. (2020). Introduction to issue 3 2020: Critical reflection. *Social Alternatives*, *39*(3), 3–4.

Maxwell, J. C. (Aug. 7, 2012). Are you really leading, or are you just taking a walk? Retrieved from https://johnmaxwell.com/blog/are-you-really-leading-or-are-you-just-taking-a-walk

Open Government Directive. (2009). Retrieved from https://obamawhitehouse.archives.gov/open/documents/open-government-directive

Stocks, C., Trevitt, C., & Hughes, J. (2018). Exploring action learning for academic development in research intensive settings. *Innovations in Education and Teaching International*, *55*, 123–132.

van der Voet, J. (2016). Change leadership and public sector organizational change: Examining the interactions of transformational leadership style and red tape. *American Review of Public Administration*, *46*(6), 660–682.

Zacher, H., & Johnson, E. (2015). Leadership and creativity in higher education. *Studies in Higher Education*, *40*, 1210–1225.

PART III
Pathways of Reflection

7
REFLECTION AS DOUBT

Mathematician and philosopher René Descartes once noted that "... in order to seek truth, it is necessary once in the course of our life, to doubt, as far as possible, of all things" (Part I, n.d.) When we are trained to believe that a concept or ideology is universally true, it can be a challenge to doubt or rethink (and perhaps even to unlearn, as introduced in Chapter 6) status quo perspectives that have become ingrained in our mindsets. Such notions may have played a critical role in shaping our worldview, including our perception of our own roles within society, but these restrictive thoughts can be unlearned through reflective practice. In this chapter, we will dissect a popular example of universal truth and consider how a reflective administrator might approach such assertions using critical thinking skills and their own ethical framework.

Family upbringing, educational experiences, and even peer influence are key factors in socialization, which factor into one's political beliefs and religious practice (Shulman & DeAndrea, 2014). The notion of universal truth derives from legal theory (Tamanaha, 2017), with adherents throughout religion and the political sphere, as well. In a nutshell, universal truth holds to the requisite or essential elements of a concept (i.e., a law, doctrine, or policy) that are considered necessary for all scenarios or applications of the conviction.

Take, for example, the crime of murder. On the surface, most people would agree that murder is wrong. However, the definition of murder and the motives that lead to taking another human's life are much less concrete. In our legal system, we have principles such as self-defense, which provide a defendant with justification for why they killed another person. Killing another person who is trying to murder you is generally recognized as an acceptable rationale for the otherwise-forbidden act of taking a life.

One caveat worth noting is that labeling a maxim as *universal* begs for rebuttal (as with the murder scenario, above). To take the example even further, what does it mean to take a life, and how is "life" defined? A seemingly simple example of saying that "murder is wrong" can morph into highly nuanced (not to mention extremely controversial) debates over subjects like euthanasia, suicide, life support, abuse, and abortion. As Tamanaha (2017) stated: "Talk about essential and necessary features is puzzling in relation to social institutions like law—based on ideas, beliefs, and actions—which come in a multitude of variations and change over time" (p. 4). Public policies often follow the trends of public perceptions, and a reflective administrator needs to be able to adapt to a changing environment.

An example of a so-called universal truth is the Golden Rule, which has long been deemed an irrefutable benchmark for interpersonal relations. John Dewey (1908) described *doubt* as "… a temporary suspense and vacillation of reactions" (p. 129); for the sake of illustration, this chapter will take a philosophical angle to explore ways in which various interpretations of the Golden Rule can demonstrate how a healthy dose of reflective doubt can help us unlearn practices and habits that are unproductive or ineffective.

Despite the Golden Rule's philosophical stature as one of (if not *the*) most widely acknowledged cultural mores, some scholars disagree whether consensus on a fundamental, global ethic statement is even possible (Burton & Goldsby, 2005). That said, no fewer than 10 world religions view some variant of the Golden Rule as a yardstick by which decisions and actions are measured (Frank, 1954; Stanglin, 2005; Wattles, 1987), and it remains an internationally understood directive. In some parts of the world, governments are structured as a theocracy, meaning that religious leaders call the shots. This makes the discussion of the Golden Rule even more apropos, because attempting to legislate morality is a tricky undertaking, yet countless government bodies have tried. Next, we will use our reflective practice tools and explore this universal truth from a variety of angles.

Standard Rendition: Do unto Others as You Would Have Them Do unto You

The standard version of the Golden Rule that children from both secular and devoutly religious homes can recite from grade school and Sunday School hearkens back to the New Testament, though the overarching concept is reflected within several cultural and religious doctrines, as noted above. The call to "Treat others as you want them to treat you" (Contemporary English Version Bible, 2005; Matthew, 7:12) transcends purely spiritual interpretations and is reiterated as a cross-cultural ethical mandate.

In each of two biblical references (Matthew, 7:12; Luke, 6:31), the Golden Rule directive is nestled within a more comprehensive passage about relating to others. The reference in Luke pertains to dealing with those perceived as enemies; in other words, even a rival's best interests should be taken into consideration if there is any hope of reconciling the relationship. The passage in Matthew expounds on the basic command to treat others as one would wish reciprocated. By adding a universal element to the statement, the Golden Rule finds application not merely in adversarial relationships, but in every interaction. The Golden Rule is so highly esteemed that the passage in Matthew described it as summarizing the entire Old Testament Jewish law and admonitions of the prophets.

John Dewey once wrote: "It is an old story that philosophers, in common with theologians and social theorists, are as sure that personal habits and interests shape their opponents' doctrines as they are that their own beliefs are 'absolutely' universal and objective in quality" (1916, p. 326). It is within this context of universal application that we turn our attention back to reflective practice. As we explored in Chapter 6, becoming reflective administrators may require temporarily suspending judgment and being willing to unlearn practices and habits that are unproductive or ineffective (Dewey, 1916).

> **MIRROR MOMENT**
>
> Empathizing with one's foes or opponents seems counterintuitive, but it is a hallmark feature of the Golden Rule. How might this attitude play out in the workplace, as we reflect upon our interactions with colleagues and/or clients who cause us frustration? How could you use reflection-in-action as you consider your interpersonal relationships in the workplace?

Inverse Interpretation: Do Not Do unto Others What You Would Not Have Them Do unto You

Saving face in front of one's peers and subordinates is a critical social element in many cultures. At the heart of maintaining honor within one's community and family lies an irrevocable sense of loyalty; in fact, the Confucian perspective of the Golden Rule links loyalty and community as a matter of moral, interpersonal relations (Wong, 1999). The inverse interpretation of the Golden Rule – also referred to as a negative interpretation or the "Silver Rule" (Swidler, 2019) – can be found in both its Western and Eastern iterations and is exemplified in the practice of saving face. To not do something to another person that one would not wish to have reciprocated is akin to not embarrassing the family with immoral behavior or not putting a leader's reputation at stake by pointing out their weaknesses in public.

These traits of loyalty and honor among peers compel a reflective administrator to consider the ripple effect of their behavior, actions, and attitudes. As noted in Chapter 2, leading from a foundation of ethical decision-making is not only a public service value but also an overarching human value. This same principle is echoed here in the inverse interpretation of the Golden Rule because we uphold the public trust when we interact with others using an ethical framework. Reciprocation is, after all, at the heart of the Golden Rule.

Economic Axiom: He Who Has the Gold Rules

In addition to the standard and inverse renditions of the Golden Rule, tangential interpretations contort the meaning further. For example, the Golden Rule—where rule means headship rather than statute—could be defined as oligarchy or the reign of the wealthy, such as the hereditary rule of rich monarchies or the exorbitant campaign spending by candidates in a democratic election. This unflattering interpretation is reinforced through the public's negative perception of the bureaucracy as a bloated, money-wasting behemoth. At a more local level, consider the stereotypically negative attitude of college faculty members toward those in administration whom they view as disconnected, or school teachers' feelings about their principals who only seem to be focused on standardized testing results.

Dewey once asked, "What will it profit a man to do this, that, and the other specific thing, if he has no clear idea of why he is doing them, no clear idea of the way they bear upon actual conditions and of the end to be reached?" (1940, p. 302). As reflective public leaders, are we willing to face this question head-on and take an honest look at ways in which we might rethink and repair the damage that has been inflicted on the public trust, not to mention within the communities and organizations in which we serve as leaders? (Dewey, 1940).

Preemptive Justification: Do unto Others before They Can Do unto You

Herein lies another variation of the Golden Rule—namely, to act preemptively and aggressively before similarly devastating action could be taken against someone. As with the economic interpretation above, this axiom paints an undesirable picture of public administration as an impersonal and inconvenient obstacle to overcome, rather than a helpful system to navigate. We will explore reflection as a component of organizational culture in more detail in Chapter 11, but this idea of instigating actions preemptively ought to give us pause to consider how we, as individual leaders, might make an impactful change on our agencies and institutions through our own personal reflective practice.

Developing Resilience

To this point, this chapter has centered on doubt and learning (or unlearning and relearning, as the case may be) what we understand to be *true* for our own lives and in the context of our professional work. As we recognize the cultural, familial, and societal influences that are sometimes at cross-purposes, we can develop resilience to navigate the changes and challenges. The varied interpretations of a universal truth described earlier in the chapter indicate ways that individuals might adapt to the same concept using different decision-making modes from their peers. Likewise, our agencies and organizations throughout the public sector and beyond can also adapt and develop resilience at a broader, institutional level.

Robb (2000) explains, "A Resilient Organization is able to sustain competitive advantage over time through its capability to do two things simultaneously: deliver excellent performance against current goals; [and to] effectively innovate and adapt to rapid, turbulent changes in markets and technologies" (p. 27). As noted previously, to doubt is not necessarily negative. Doubting causes us to rethink, broaden our perspectives, and to challenge the status quo. This is important not only at the individual level but also systematically within an organization.

The stereotypical image of the public sector, a.k.a., the bureaucracy, coincides with the portrait of what Robb (2000) describes as a performance-oriented organization. In Chapter 1, we looked at foundational theories and historical perspectives of the bureaucracy, which largely focused on efficiency of operations, more so than personnel development. The early bureaucracy (and even the modern iteration, to some extent) was judged by quantifiable metrics and other hard skills, rather than soft skills like customer service. This type of performance-oriented mindset is "… all about maintaining equilibrium, focus and action within the current system, while adaptation skills are all about creating dis-equilibrium, exploration of new systems, and creating the safety and support needed for change" (p. 30). (This imbalance between processes of the past, current expectations, and future goals can also contribute to the job satisfaction triggers for burnout that we will look at in more depth in Chapter 10.)

MIRROR MOMENT

What does your agency or organization look like, given the equilibrium context described above? What outdated policies and procedures are still in place, simply because that's the way we've always done it? How might you engage with decision-makers to shift the perspective?

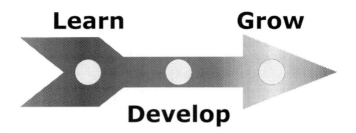

FIGURE 7.1 A resilient organization is one that learns, develops, and grows together

Speaking about performance-driven organizations, in particular, Robb (2000) noted, "Their bureaucratic, political structures serve to cope with anxiety and stress primarily by controlling it or suppressing it in the interests of preserving order and the status quo" (p. 28). More innovative, risk-taking, adaption-driven organizations, on the other hand, "... are extremely responsive but often have difficulties with inconsistent performance, unstable processes, and creating stable formulas for success" (p. 28). Resilient organizations, on the other hand, represent a hybrid blend of the performance-driven and adaptation-driven models, with a common foundation to unite the two perspectives. Although these entities are varied in structure and size, and they represent organizations and corporations across both the public and private sectors, resilient organizations tend to share certain characteristics (Figure 7.1). They are not afraid to

- *Create* structure, and to *dissolve* it;
- Provide *safety* (not necessarily security or stability) in the midst of change;
- Manage the emotional consequences of continuous transformation and change: anxiety and grief;
- Learn, develop and grow.

p. 27

A reflective administrator seeking to build a resilient organization cannot be reticent to challenge the status quo, as we discussed in Chapter 6. This might mean creating new units within the institution in response to growth trends, or perhaps combining low-performing or under-enrolled units to better utilize resources. It could also mean adding term limits for board members to encourage fresh perspectives and new ideas. The creation and dissolution of structure ought to be part of our continuous improvement efforts as reflective administrators. Robb adds this clarification to distinguish resilient organizations from performance-driven ones, in particular: "Resilient Organizations, on the other hand, see themselves as living communities with an economic/ task responsibility, a subtle but profound shift in emphasis ... This helps to foster the ability to let go of outmoded structures, perspectives, strategies or behavioral styles" (p. 31).

Effective leaders within resilient organizations recognize that in many cases – particularly within the public sector – we are a service industry. The budgets for colleges and universities, municipal and county governments, and even many non-profit organizations are heavily tilted toward human resource expenditures. Most public agencies do not manufacture or sell a product; they provide services, and those services are implemented by people. When change is necessary within an organization, a common knee-jerk reaction among employees is to fret about the security of their jobs. Let's look back on the example above about an institution combining under-performing departments. One way that a reflective administrator could provide a sense of safety in that scenario is to communicate openly with the affected departments about what changes (if any) will be coming down the pike, in terms of personnel cuts. Perhaps any unnecessary positions will simply be handled through attrition – that is, not filling a position once it is vacated. Reductions in personnel do not necessarily mean layoffs, but the onus falls on the leadership to offer that reassurance to the team.

Closely related to providing a sense of safety is managing the emotional fallout that tends to happen during seasons of organizational change. A reflective administrator can help assuage those feelings and squash rumors before they spread by engaging in regular and transparent communication. Leaders of a resilient organization will acknowledge the concerns they hear and recognize that change is difficult for many people, while also delivering a forward-looking message of hope and positivity for the institution or agency.

The final component of a resilient organization (and the reflective administrators within it) is that they continue to learn from best practices and new research; they encourage professional development and seek opportunities to do so for themselves, and they pursue growth at the individual, unit, and organizational level. Reflective administrators and resilient organizations are never satisfied with the status quo because they are on a pathway of constant improvement.

Regardless of how stereotypical and unfair the accusation may be, the public sector often has a negative reputation as being like the performance-driven organization that Robb described: impersonal and rote with regard to customer service. Reflective public administrators can learn to harness doubt as a healthy way of questioning how their interactions are received by clients. As we seek to rethink and relearn through reflective doubt, we can adjust our approach to public service by recognizing our street-level bureaucratic discretion and consider how our actions and attitudes may affect those we serve and the organizations within which we work. As these changes take hold at a personal level, they can begin to influence our organizations and communities, as well.

What Is True and What Is Right?

Earlier, we looked at various interpretations of the Golden Rule as a so-called universal truth. We began to unpack how the idea of universality is not as clear-cut as it may seem; rather, it is contingent upon individual circumstances and motives. We then turned our attention to the concept of resilience and the necessity to engage in doubt and challenge the status quo – both internally and within our organizations. Next, we will examine our own value systems and consider the influences on our worldviews of which we might not even yet be aware.

As we explored in this chapter, just because a perspective may have been ingrained in us from youth as "true" doesn't necessarily make it *right*. The socializations we inherited through our upbringing become part of our vantage points, whether we realize it or not. The basis of implicit bias, after all, is a worldview that is implied even if not expressed overtly. In other words, the bias is planted into the soil from which our social constructs grow. Khan (2017) describes it this way: "Implicit bias involves three basic steps: the mental recognition or construction of a social group; the association of a stereotype with that group; and the layering of a positive or negative association or attitude on top of the stereotype" (p. 25).

The Declaration of Independence of the United States of America includes the phrase: "We hold these truths to be self-evident, that all men are created equal …" Let's unpack this claim of apparent equality by considering that a myriad of examples have flooded the news in recent years, particularly in the U.S., about biases among law enforcement officers. Khan (2017) explains, "It is not just about equal protection under the law: it is about the substantive constitutional value of not being devalued and humiliated by the state on the basis of the fundamental aspect of one's identity" (p. 233). (Does this sound a bit like the inverse interpretation of the Golden Rule from earlier?) If all persons are inherently equal at their core, then how might those who have invested their careers in protecting the peace also guard against their own biases?

The first step in identifying our own implicit biases is recognizing that we actually have them. It would be willfully ignorant of any of us to deny that we have any biases, whatsoever. In the case of our law enforcement example, an officer might begin by acknowledging that although a disproportionate number of traffic stops, arrests, and/or convictions might sway toward particular demographics, the root causes of these problems might very well be more systemic than they may have given consideration toward, because they previously looked at the issues from an insulated worldview.

None of us are beyond reproach, and as Khan (2017) suggested, "We must acknowledge racism's past power and continuing salience in our world. And we must engage it forthrightly, without apology, without fear of offending those who would rather not see. Only in this way can we hope to change the story we tell ourselves about race, racism, and justice" (p. 234). A reflective administrator needs to be someone who is willing to take an honest look in the mirror and use their reflection-for-action skills to make adjustments toward a more positive future – both personally and as an influence on their organizations.

> **MIRROR MOMENT**
>
> Given what you have read in this chapter regarding reflective practice as doubt and as a moral compass, what suggestions might you offer to a law enforcement officer who is trying to grapple with their implicit biases on the job?

Our Stories and Reflective Practice

Our personal human information and memories are not housed in a vault; they are contained in our brain as stories. Humans have a retention system of information that exists in narrative patterns and forms. We do not assign information and memories a labeled space or particular section in a cabinet within our memories. We arrive at a certain memory that often is determined by trigger factors such as smell, facial features, sound, food, and sense of detail. The narrative of our memory system for understanding, remembering, and communicating are at the center of how we make sense of our relationships (Bolton, 2005). People's lives are structured and ordered by the stories in which our interactions and understandings are embedded, told and retold daily through actions, memories, thoughts, dreams, habits, beliefs, speech, and behavior patterns.

In life, people tell and retell stories, and by doing so, they contribute to the larger social context of a community, company, educational institution, etc. It is a natural process that repeats and is as common as breathing. Scholar and anthropologist James McDonald (2022) noted that this perspective is common among the Humanities professions, in that "… human thought is crafted in terms of stories, and those stories construct our reality." Given that stories are part of the scaffolding that build our worldviews, a reflective administrator must practice listening to others and themselves. Reflection and talking together helps with the development of effective listening skills; in fact, a key element to our entire discussion of reflective practice is the importance of developing strong listening skills.

Reflective practice is built upon the experience each practitioner brings to the environment of work, school, business, or home. All of us need to be aware of the history, opinions, and knowledge that our colleagues bring in order to establish relationships that establish the foundation for reflective practice. With reflective practice, we often think of asking ourselves questions, but in some contexts, it is also important to the work of reflective practice to engage others in the questioning. In the work environment, for example, questions directed toward colleagues might include *How could I have done it better? Do you think the presentation of the material met the needs of the team?* The questioning process can lead to taking responsibility within the reflective practice phases in-action, on-action, and for-action. Bolton (2005) put it this way: "In order to take responsibility for professional actions, and some of the actions of others, we need clearer perception of how we build our world, and how others build it around us - its narrative and metamorphic structures and content. This perception will enable, necessitate even, change and development" (274).

Bolton insists that practitioners of reflective practice are, by necessity, change agents as they engage in effective reflection, explore experience, values, and professional identities, and express aspects within certain personal and professional bounds which they expect to be respected. They must be open to having understandings challenged, willing to have beliefs questioned, and courageous in discovering aspects underlying and affecting daily behavior, of which they were previously unaware. Reflective administrators are willing to unearth their own implicit biases and confront systemic problem areas within their organizations, as well.

Case Study

As we explored above, resilient organizations are able to "... effectively innovate and adapt to rapid, turbulent changes in markets and technologies" (Robb, 2000, p. 27). One of the most complicated times in recent memory when agencies and institutions across the globe were forced to pivot abruptly occurred in early 2020, as the COVID-19 pandemic spread. Colleges and universities had to quickly switch gears from face-to-face classroom delivery to an online modality. Non-profit organizations that provided on-site or group services were required to think creatively about how to meet clients' needs in a safe and socially distanced manner. Visitations at hospitals, jails, nursing homes, and tourist sites were halted. Many county courthouses even shifted to virtual hearings during this time. In short, agencies and organizations throughout the public sector (not to mention the corporate world, as well) had to turn on a dime to adapt to factors outside of their control. The pandemic caused us to question business as usual and begin to rethink how we operate on a daily basis.

Robb's (2000) description of a resilient organization is one that is adaptive to structural changes; focused on garnering a sense of safety within the agency; mindful of employees' (and clients') emotional responses to change; and willing to learn from past and current experiences in order to grow. In light of these criteria, how would you assess your institution's or organization's response to the pandemic?

- Was the executive leadership team open to the changes that needed to occur, in the moment?
- Did the employees, students, volunteers, and other stakeholders feel a sense of security and direction, even amid the agency's efforts to navigate the unknown?
- How has the organization changed permanently (if at all) since the early days of the pandemic? Have any of the adaptations that were implemented then actually stayed in place because they turned out to be positive moves for the organization?
- What could/should the institution or agency have done differently, in retrospect?

Conclusion

Reflective practice compels us to enter a state of doubt and be willing to reconsider practices and attitudes that we once may have believed to be universally true. Noted entertainer, producer, and director Amy Poehler echoed this self-awareness process in her book, *Yes Please*, saying, "It takes years as a woman to unlearn what you have been taught to be sorry for. It takes years to find your voice and seize your real estate" (2015, p. 65). These are important skills for any public service professional to keep in their toolbox. In the following chapter, we will begin to unpack the strengths that each of us bring into our workplace environments and explore how we can hone these skills to enhance our professional growth.

References

Bolton, G. (2005). Taking responsibility for our stories: In reflective practice, action learning, and Socratic dialogue. *Teaching in Higher Education, 10*(2), 271–280. doi:10.1080/1356251052000341048.

Burton, B. K., & Goldsby, M. (2005). The golden rule and business ethics: An examination. *Journal of Business Ethics, 56*, 371–383. doi:10.1007/s10551-004-4185-7.

Contemporary English Version Bible. (2005). New York: American Bible Society.

Descartes, R. (n.d.). *Selections from the principles of philosophy*. Translated by John Veitch. Part I (I). Retrieved from http://www.classicallibrary.org/descartes/principles/01.htm

Dewey, J. (1908) Does reality possess practical character? In L. A. Hickman & T. M. Alexander (Eds.), *The essential Dewey, vol. 1: Pragmatism, education, democracy* (p. 129). Bloomington, IN: Indiana University Press.

Dewey, J. (1916). *Essays in experimental logic*. Chicago, IL: The University of Chicago Press.

Dewey, J. (1940) *Education today.* New York: G. P. Putnam's Sons.
Frank, R. (1954). The golden rule—In ten religions. *The Clearing House, 28*(5): 276. Retrieved from www.jstor.org/stable/30176251
Khan, J. (2017). *Race on the brain: What implicit bias gets wrong about the struggle for racial justice* (p. 25). New York: Columbia Press.
McDonald, J. H. (2022). Seduced by story [Review of the book *Seduced by Story: The Use and Abuse of Narrative*, by P. Brooks]. *New York Journal of Books.* Retrieved from https://www.nyjournalofbooks.com/book-review/seduced-story
Poehler, A. (2015). *Yes please.* New York: Dey Street Books.
Robb, D. (2000). Building resilient organizations. *OD Practitioner, 32(3)*, 27–32.
Shulman, H. C., & DeAndrea, D. C. (2014). Predicting success: Revisiting assumptions about family political socialization. *Communication Monographs, 81*(3), 386–406.
Stanglin, Keith D. (2005). The historical connection between the golden rule and the second greatest love command. The Journal of Religious Ethics, 33(2), 357–371. Retrieved from www.jstor.org/stable/40015310
Swidler, L. (2019). The "golden rule": The "best rule". *Journal of Ecumenical Studies, 54*(2), 279–288. doi:10.1353/ecu.2019.0008.
Tamanaha, B. Z. (2017). Necessary and universal truths about law? *Ratio Juris, 30*(1), 3–24.
Wattles, J. (1987). Levels of meaning in the golden rule. The Journal of Religious Ethics, 15(1): 106–129. Retrieved from www.jstor.org/stable/40015055
Wong, Q. J. (1999). The golden rule and interpersonal care: From a confucian perspective. *Philosophy East and West, 49*(4): 415–438. Retrieved from www.jstor.org/stable/1399946

8
REFLECTION AS SELF-ANALYSIS

Constructive criticism, directed both internally and externally, is necessary to allow a reflective practice to accomplish its full work. After all, it would be futile to regard reflection as simply a pat on the back with no room for learning from errors or aiming to grow professionally. However, a prolonged focus on solely negative aspects is not the goal here. In this chapter, we will look at professional growth from a strengths perspective with reflective practice at the core.

The popularity of the strengths perspective derives from social work scholars and practitioners in the late-1980s. Then-dean of the School of Social Welfare at the University of Kansas, Ann Weick, along with her colleagues, is credited with formalizing this strengths-based approach and naming it the strengths perspective (KU School of Social Welfare, 2022). Researchers during that era realized that the prevailing attention given to problem-solving had inadvertently pigeonholed the helping professions into focusing primarily on negative traits. (People have problems, and problems need to be fixed; therefore, let's zero in on those issues.) The strengths perspective, by contrast, does not ignore problems but intentionally seeks to identify and highlight strong suits. Researcher Charles Rapp (1988) explained it this way: "The strengths perspective is an alternative to a preoccupation with negative aspects of people and society ..." (p. 2).

This draw toward problems over possibilities is certainly not limited to the social work profession; the public sector is riddled with examples of negativity. Consider the stereotypical reputation of public administration where *bureaucracy* is an inherently unpleasant term that conjures up imagery of red tape and poor customer service. Think of the difference in how the public

DOI: 10.4324/9781003270775-12

stereotypically views firefighters and police officers: One is naturally helpful and service-oriented, while the other is setting a speed trap so they can write you a ticket. These persistent stereotypes, of course, are not always fair or even accurate.

Besides the challenge of stereotypes toward various professions, the culture of a workplace is another important consideration, as to whether change is encouraged (or even permitted to be discussed). Adult learning scholar Stephen Brookfield (1987) offered this scenario: "Sometimes the only reason for workers to challenge existing workplace norms is some kind of failure or major disaster at the workplace. In the aftermath of workplace disasters, a critical questioning of workplace practices and previously unexamined workplace norms is often initiated" (p. 137).

We do not want to wait for a catastrophe to compel us to change, but adjusting this perspective and eliminating negativity requires systemic adjustments. Weick (1989) elaborated, "Problem-based assessments encourage individualistic rather than social-environmental explanations of human problems" (p. 351). As reflective administrators, we must look beyond individual faults or limitations and consider how the collective efforts of our teams, units, and even communities might be channeled in a positive manner to improve our organizations. With the strengths perspective as a foundation, we will turn our attention to harnessing these tools gleaned from the social work profession and adapting them to the public sector more broadly.

What Are Strengths?

Like personalities and physical traits, strengths manifest in a variety of ways among individuals, and it is our potential that makes us uniquely human. Weick (1989) explained, "All people possess a wide range of talents, abilities, capacities, skills, resources, and aspirations. No matter how little or how much may be expressed at one time, a belief in human potential is tied to the notion that people have untapped, undetermined reservoirs of mental, physical, emotional, social, and spiritual abilities that can be expressed. The presence of this capacity for continued growth and heightened well-being means that people must be accorded the respect that this power deserves" (p. 352).

Saleebey (2002) defined personal strengths through a series of introspective considerations, beginning with what people have discovered about themselves. To reiterate, this concept stems from a therapeutic approach, but our goal in this chapter is to explore how these principles might be applied more broadly to the public sector workforce, as well as professional development at an individual level. As a reflective administrator, you might have learned things about yourself over time, such as how you interact with colleagues most effectively, how you best manage your time, or how you successfully tackle new projects. These traits are your strengths!

Reflection as Self-Analysis **103**

FIGURE 8.1 Using the strengths perspective

Another factor to consider, as we investigate our own strengths, is your personal virtues or the moral compass through which you view the world, as we discussed in Chapter 7. Saleebey echoed the notion that what we have learned about the world around us contributes to our toolbox of strengths, as well. Our worldview is only as broad as our lived experiences or our willingness to learn from others' lived experiences. Broadening one's scope of understanding about the society in which we live is an important strength for a reflective administrator to hone. Personal talents, certainly, fall into the category of one's strengths, as well. Saleebey (2002) also draws attention to points of personal pride, cultural and spiritual influences, as well as one's community network or support system as potential strengths (Figure 8.1).

Elements of Strengths

According to Saleebey (2002), strengths-based practice consists of four important elements (p. 90). We will consider each in turn, with an adaptive twist to apply the principles from the social work profession to a variety of workplace environments:

1. *Acknowledge the pain.* In a therapeutic context, this means to guide clients through a process of facing their trauma – both past and present – in an

effort to help them move forward. The strengths perspective comes into play as the individual begins to identify take-aways from painful experiences that can help them to be more resilient going forward. Consider how a similar approach might be adapted to the public sector workplace: Instead of allowing a disgruntled colleague to derail a meeting with negativity, a reflective administrator might redirect the dialogue to acknowledge frustrations (long-standing within the organization and/or current concerns), then steer the conversation to how the individuals and organization, as a whole, can learn and grow from those experiences.

2. *Stimulate the discourse and narratives of resilience and strength.* A social worker may help a client spot their own abilities and successes through a process. Saleebey describes as mirroring, where the worker reframes the client's accomplishments in a way that aids them in seeing beyond their personal doubts. Likewise, a reflective administrator can contribute to a culture of positivity within the workplace by seeking out opportunities to spotlight others' strengths. Just as verbal affirmations may help to build trust within a therapeutic relationship between worker and client, so might such acknowledgments also support a more trusting environment among colleagues.

3. *Act in context: education, action, advocacy, lineage.* Collaboration and continuity are key factors in implementing a strengths perspective within the social work profession. These efforts are not intended to be one-off attempts or singular experiences. As we apply these concepts to the public sector workplace, as well, it is important to note that identifying strengths individually and collectively is an ongoing effort; we are on a trajectory of continuous improvement.

4. *Move toward normalizing and capitalizing on one's strengths.* Because drawing attention to one's own strengths may be a foreign concept to many, a strategy within the social work profession is to help clients normalize the strengths perspective and challenge them to be resourceful as they progress on their own. An association to the field of public service may look like a reflective administrator who empowers their team to take on new responsibilities that stretch their comfort zones, all the while helping individuals within the organization to recognize how their unique skills and abilities contribute to the overall mission.

> **MIRROR MOMENT**
>
> Considering Saleebey's four elements of strengths-based practice, how might you apply these concepts to your specific workplace, organization, or institution?

Each of the four elements described above provide an invitation for individuals to begin the process of constructive critique through reflective practice. Critical reflection is more than just a thinking exercise; it is a call to action. As Welsh and Dehler explain, "Critical reflection draws attention to the difference between doing something because 'that's what we do' and doing something because it is necessary and possible in the situation" (2013, p. 794). As we become aware of our own strengths and those within our teams, we can zero in on strategies to apply our collective strengths in ways that are effective and meaningful for each unique agency or organization.

The Language of Critique

Welsh and Dehler align reflective criticism with the experiences of multilingual individuals, noting that "… being multiliterate means appreciating differences in language – as one translates, one essentially turns the language back on itself; the process of negotiating identity similarly entails reflexivity, turning one identity on another" (2013, p. 795). They note that being knowledgeable of multiple languages opens the doors to better understanding of diverse perspectives and learning from each other's differences. That said, the term *literacy* may also be applied in a broader sense to include more than linguistics, such as the language of one's strengths. Being able to engage with each other's strength-languages is a key element for collaboration, whether the scenario takes place in the classroom or the boardroom.

Welsh and Dehler go on to describe the dynamics within educational settings where individuals exhibit interpersonal multiliteracy by explaining, "In each process, students are engaging in critical reflection on a collective, rather than individual, basis. As positions are critiqued, some meanings and values become dominant; others become marginalized or negated" (2013, p. 795). This important distinction between constructive criticism geared toward a group or systematic level, rather than directed at individuals, dovetails with Weick's perspective mentioned previously in this chapter.

Critique does not have to be inherently negative; on the contrary, the reflective administrator considers constructive criticism with an eye toward organizational improvement. It is important that critique be handled head-on, not brushed under the rug. "To confront means to hold someone accountable," Patterson, Greeny, McMillan, and Switzler (2005) explains: "Although the term can sound abrasive, that's not what we have in mind. In fact, when confrontations are handled correctly, both parties talk openly and honestly. Both are candid and respectful" (p. 4). Being frank and focused on systems over individuals can aid reflective leaders in facilitating positive change within their organizations.

Being willing to offer (and accept) critique and engage in necessary confrontation are vital for reflective administrators to be able to initiate change in their organizations. Brookfield noted, "Fostering critical thinking at the workplace is something we should support not simply because of the benefit to be derived from higher productivity and greater worker satisfaction; rather, we should recognize the opportunity to exercise critical thought at the workplace as one of the chief ways in which we affirm our identities" (1987, p. 161).

Empowerment Evaluation

Chapter 6 introduced the benefits of empowerment leadership. With the notion of continuous improvement in mind, we will now turn our attention to empowerment evaluation as one more strategy to consider. Self-determination serves as the basis for empowerment evaluation, which meshes with the current discussion regarding the strengths perspective. At its core, self-determination focuses on one's ability to navigate their chosen path in life, and in order to accomplish this goal, one must be in tune with their own capabilities or strengths (Fetterman, Kaftarian, & Wandersman, 1996).

What if one's strengths aren't readily apparent? Saleebey suggests five questions to ask to help identify strengths that might otherwise be overlooked (2002, p. 89):

- Survival – How have you overcome challenges that have arisen, and what did you discover about yourself during those trials?
- Support – Who are your go-to people or groups, and what makes them reliable, compared to others who are not in your support network?
- Exception – What moments or chapters in your life would you like to press pause and relish in the experience a while longer? What made those episodes particularly special?
- Possibility – What daydreams or goals do you hope to achieve? What types of activities do you love to do the most?
- Esteem – If someone bragged about you to someone else, what would they say? What aspects of your life are you most proud of, personally?

In the social work context, Saleebey's questions would likely be posed to a client to consider holistically about their life. However, since the focus of this chapter is on adapting the strengths perspective for professional growth, let's reframe the five inquiries through a workplace lens:

- Survival – Consider an obstacle that you have encountered on the job. How were you able to overcome the hurdle, and what did you learn about yourself during the process?
- Support – Among your co-workers, who are the ones you can always count on to pull their weight on a project? What characteristics make them your go-to colleagues, compared to others who are not as reliable?

- Exception – Think of a top-notch day or a project at work that turned out exceptionally well. What made that situation stand out so positively to you?
- Possibility – What types of tasks or projects do you enjoy tackling at work? What is a professional goal that you would especially like to accomplish?
- Esteem – If someone were to put in a good word about you to your supervisor, what might they say? What elements of your job are you particularly proud of, speaking for yourself?

Recognizing our own strengths allows us to participate in empowerment evaluation, as we learn more about ourselves through self-analysis. Reframing Saleebey's strengths-finding questions from the vantage point of the workplace can aid not only in identifying strengths but also performance evaluations and goal setting. Imagine what our organizations, agencies, and institutions would look like if we framed annual performance reviews from a strengths perspective and set goals for ourselves and our teams that hinged on each other's assets and positive traits, rather than simply problem-solving?

Speaking about the strengths perspective in varied contexts, social work practitioner and educator Tim Davis explained: "It's deeper than therapeutic; it's a worldview of how you see humanity" (Davis, personal communication, September 29, 2002). Regardless of whether a strengths assessment is conducted in a therapeutic setting or workplace environment, Rapp (1998) noted that it is not an activity that should be imposed upon someone; on the contrary, the individual being evaluated should play an active role in the process. The strengths perspective, itself, becomes an element of the evaluation. Davis elaborated, "It's not a technique but integrated into the way you assess" (Davis, personal communication, September 29, 2002). In essence, implementing a strengths perspective is much like the foundational principles of reflective practice: It becomes woven into one's learning and decision-making process. In this manner, self-evaluation becomes a form of advocacy.

Fetterman (1996) describes the process of annual performance evaluations as one example of advocacy through evaluation, in that an employee appraises their own performance on the job and presents their findings to their supervisor as justification for a positive review (p. 13). Empowerment evaluation is not designed to be limited to one-on-one application, however. Fetterman goes on to explain, "Empowerment evaluation is necessarily a collaborative group activity, not an individual pursuit. An evaluator does not and cannot empower anyone; people empower themselves, often with assistance and coaching. This process is fundamentally democratic. It invites (if not demands) participation, examining issues of concern to the entire community in an open forum" (p. 5).

> **MIRROR MOMENT**
>
> Thinking about both the personal and workplace versions of Saleebey's five questions for bringing strengths to light, what overlaps did you notice in your own responses? What about contrasts? Did you find that you exhibit any different strengths on a personal front than you do at work? What might you focus on in either context to continue developing those strengths?

As reflective administrators seek to improve the culture of their organizations, they need to engage other stakeholders in the effort. Self-evaluation can help empower a team or entire organization to evaluate itself for strategic planning purposes through focus groups and brainstorming sessions. Four specific steps can aid us in this cooperative evaluation effort (adapted from Fetterman et al., 1996):

- *Taking stock.* Thinking back to previous chapters where we discussed the three types of reflective practice, this step falls under the category of reflection-on-action. As we take stock of the organization's current culture, we consider historical trends and decision-making patterns that have brought the organization to its present state.
- *Setting goals and developing strategies.* These two steps go hand-in-hand as examples of reflection-for-action. Strategic goal setting is inherently forward-thinking and allows us to use reflective practice as a planning tool for the future.
- *Documenting progress.* Lastly, we see here an example of reflection-in-action, as we track and evaluate our efforts in real time. Recording progress toward our goals, in turn, informs our ability to take stock in how far we've come, and the cycle continues on our trajectory of ongoing improvement.

Strengths Perspective as a Catalyst for Change

We have looked at the strengths perspective as an evaluative tool, but now let's explore how we can apply these same concepts to affect positive change at the organizational level and even within the community, at large. Roff (2004) describes the strengths perspective as "… the catalyst that harnesses the creative power of communities in an effort to create social change" (p. 203). The work of nonprofit organizations and public sector agencies centers on their mission. At their optimal functioning level, these entities can leave a footprint on their communities by filling gaps and meeting needs that might otherwise go unaddressed. Thus far, we have considered the strengths perspective as a tool for personal, professional growth, but the positive impact of public sector agencies could be viewed as an organizational level, or collective, strength.

Ultimately, the tools we develop using the strengths perspective help us to become "... capable of problem-solving in the cultural context" (Roff, 2004, p. 211). We will dig more deeply into reflective practice as a key component to organizational culture in Chapter 11, but for now, we will focus on the mission-centered purpose of the public and nonprofit sector and explore how the strengths perspective might reveal real-world application well beyond its origins within the social work profession.

For starters, let's consider the example of nongovernmental organizations. These organizations exist independently from government agencies and function similarly to traditional nonprofit organizations. They tend to be volunteer-centric, charitable organizations with a focus on advocacy, economic development, and other humanitarian purposes related to a specific issue or population. Speaking of nonprofit work as the starting point for community improvement, Roff (2004) explained, "Nongovernmental organizations offer opportunities for community-led, issue-driven efforts towards social change" (p. 203). Roff also noted that the mission-driven focus of nongovernmental organizations mirrors the core values of the social work profession, namely: "self-determination, the central importance of human relationships, [and] the need to challenge social injustice" (p. 211).

MIRROR MOMENT

What is the mission statement for your workplace? What would you consider to be the top three strengths of the organization, as a whole? How do your personal strengths fit into the agency's mission?

If the strengths perspective can help to channel the collective efforts of a community to influence social change, then we ought to begin thinking critically about ways in which we can put our own strengths into action within our workplaces – whether in the traditional public sector, a nonprofit organization, or even the private sector. Just as we considered reflective practice using the strengths perspective as a professional development tool at an individual level, we can also adapt that mindset to evaluating and improving the agencies and institutions in which we work.

Roff noted, "Students of social work need to think collectively, always with an eye towards mobilizing and building on the natural helping networks available in a community" (2004, p. 211). Regardless of our particular area of discipline, the sentiment holds true that public service professionals from any field ought to keep their collective agencies or institutions in the forefront of their minds as they seek out ways to invest their strengths and skills to help fulfill the organization's mission.

Case Study

Throughout this chapter, we have kept an eye on learning our personal strengths, honing and implementing them in professional practice, and growing them over time for the betterment of not only our own careers, but also the organizations in which we serve. But, what if we find ourselves in the situation of needing to rein in those same skills?

A final-semester nursing student serves as a mentor to other nurse assistants at a local hospital. They have conducted clinical rotations throughout various specialty disciplines of the field and have gained a reputation as a quick study, someone who gets things done efficiently and accurately, as well as a trustworthy colleague to help train others. The nursing student has finished their coursework with flying colors and is now in the limbo period of studying and waiting to take the state licensure exam to earn their official credentials.

Let's consider two scenarios for our soon-to-be registered nurse, in light of this chapter's focus on the strengths perspective:

1. When mentoring a new nurse aid, the nursing student feels the need to stand back and let the inexperienced trainee struggle through processes as part of their own learning curve. In what context(s) should our nursing student intervene to impart their own know-how (if at all), without inhibiting the newbie's training experience? What is the tipping point between exercising your own strengths and precluding someone else from discovering theirs?
2. Even as an aid, the nursing student often finds themselves in situations where they know how to perform functions safely and correctly, but the tasks are beyond the scope of their legal responsibilities as a nurse aid. How might our nursing student utilize and/or adapt their skills, given the boundaries of their current capabilities?

Considering your own field of expertise, think of a situation where someone else has lent their skills and insights in a training capacity to help you grow professionally. Have you had the opportunity to pay that effort forward to others who've come behind you? If so, how did that scenario play out? If not, how might you purposely look for ways to invest your strengths to help train the next generation of professionals within your organization or even your discipline, at large?

Conclusion

As we have unpacked in this chapter, it could be valuable to view our own professional development journeys through a strengths perspective lens. However, as reflective administrators, we also need to be mindful of our interactions with internal and external stakeholders. (Are we viewing them through the same lens as we evaluate ourselves?) Regardless of your job title, you have the capacity to lead from whatever position you hold, and that also goes for influencing those who come behind you on their journeys. With this idea of training up others in mind, we will turn our attention in the next chapter to reflective practice in the university classroom setting. There, we will look at the process of preparing future public service leaders by helping them translate theoretical concepts into real-world application.

References

Brookfield, S. D. (1987). *Developing critical thinkers: Challenging adults to explore alternative ways of thinking and acting.* San Francisco, CA: Josey-Bass Publishers.

Fetterman, D. M., Kaftarian, S. J., & Wandersman, A. (Eds.). (1996). *Empowerment evaluation: Knowledge and tools for self-assessment and accountability.* Thousand Oaks, CA: Sage Publications.

KU School of Social Welfare. (2022). University of Kansas. *History of strengths perspective at KU.* Retrieved from https://socwel.ku.edu/history-strengths-perspective

Patterson, K., Greeny, J., McMillan, R., & Switzler, R. (2005). *Crucial confrontations: Tools for resolving broken promises, violated expectations, and bad behavior.* New York: McGraw-Hill.

Rapp, C. A. (1998). *The strengths model: Case management with people suffering from severe and persistent mental illness.* New York: Oxford University Press.

Roff, S. (2004). Nongovernmental organizations: The strengths perspective at work. *International Social Work, 47*(2), 202–212.

Saleebey, D. (2002). *The strengths perspective in social work practice.* Boston, MA: Allyn and Bacon.

Weick, A. (1989). A strengths perspective for social work practice. *Social Work, 34*(4), 350–354.

Welsh, M., & Dehler, G. (2013). Combining critical reflection and design thinking to develop integrative learners. *Journal of Management Education, 37*(6), 771–802.

9
REFLECTION AS PREPARATION

A common and essential goal of many educators is to develop meaningful, enduring practices that support continuous learning and growth for their students as future professionals. Reflection can be a lens into the world of lifelong practice and professional development leading to understanding and revision in thinking. This revision is essential in skill acquisition in any profession as one continues to evolve within a career. All must remember that professions include more than the development of competencies. Key elements such as socialization within roles, identities, and dispositions are also required within a profession. Reflective practice is one professional practice that students can learn through interactions with colleagues within their academic programs. An important challenge is how to develop this tool in a significant way that the practice continues beyond the formal classroom into their profession.

As the journey of moving from reflective theory into practice unfolds, questions that must be considered by instructors include:

- What opportunities to reflect are we providing for students across the subject area curriculum?
- How do the opportunities support students as they grow in their ability to engage in advanced levels of reflection?

Through deep examination of the course curriculum and our students' needs, we are able to create and evoke learning that promotes both practice and development, allowing educators an opportunity to provide support for authentic exploration of experiential learning and its application to reflection.

DOI: 10.4324/9781003270775-13

Intersection of Theory and Practice: Moving from Understanding to Application

Reflection is an invitation to originate ideas using the concepts of open-mindedness, accountability, and enthusiasm to frame a situation or experience. Reflection can be interpreted as thinking in new ways while viewing things from different perspectives. According to Allen et al. (2018), the primary goals of reflective practice are to link theory and application, and challenge students to incorporate what they learned in the classroom setting into their lived experiences. In the everyday process of meaning-making and problem-solving, reflective theories explain that we learn procedural knowledge (how to do things or solve problems) and propositional knowledge (what things mean) through reflecting on experiences. But in critical reflection people question how they framed the problem in the first place. Even if no apparent problem exists, the thoughtful practitioner questions situations, asking why things are the way they are, why events unfold in the way they do.

Foley (2008) suggested that people also reflect critically to problematize their own actions, asking questions like: Why did I do what I did? What beliefs inform my practice, and how are these beliefs helping or hindering my work? Theory provides a solid foundation that can be trusted as a system of principles are adopted. Translating theory into practice can follow a deductive process, using analysis one can determine principles that are most relevant for the instructional development of reflective learning. After identifying aspects of the theory which include three or four principles, we then move to the discussion phase, followed by the refinement and formation phases. These steps begin to shape the principles for application and delivery. Each step requires the participation of colleagues and professionals engaged with reflective learning to secure feedback, which aids the application process.

Reflective learning is the production of a learning process that is not primarily centered around an instructor's role, rather it's focused on the multidisciplinary nature of problems, peer assessment, and the development of interpersonal skills with a goal of acquiring knowledge on all possible outcomes. This type of learning engagement requires an interactive bridge between theory and practice. The evolution of reflective learning is a never-ending process. It gives students responsibility for their own learning because they become active agents as theory, practice, and application engage.

> **MIRROR MOMENT**
>
> Reflective practice encourages practitioners to think in new ways and develop perspectives that are outside the realm of the status quo. How

> does the intersection of theory and practice support each phase of reflective practice (In-action, On-Action, and For-Action) with new interpretations of existing goals, beliefs, and values?

Experiential Learning Reflections as Preparation for the Workforce

Educators have common and important goals to achieve. One of the fundamental goals is to engage their students in learning that assists in mastery of tips, tools, and techniques that lead to lifelong practices that support repeated, ongoing learning. All of these efforts combine to encourage individual and collective continuous growth as professionals. Reflective practice provides a space for observations, experiences, and the sharing of knowledge within an environment that supports the formation of plans, steps, and structure for future actions. An important and necessary step toward application is the way instructors create a domain that encourages development, support, and the courage to let go of previously held beliefs while tolerating the ambiguity of rethinking their perspectives.

Reflecting on and evaluating multiple perspectives can support students in finding their own voices and identities. Consistent and clear terminology and expectations across subject requirements that intentionally align instruction and curriculum, allows for the construction of valuable working definitions of reflection for students and instructors. At several points during a semester, instructors should engage in face-to-face peer group discussions to reflect on student progress. Feedback is an important occurrence within reflective learning, focusing on presentation of divergent perspectives offered during class interactions and after assignments.

This engagement helps establish the use of reflection within professional environments, providing an orientation to Donald Schön's (1987) "Reflection on Seeing As," which encourages practitioners to develop new hypotheses based on reflection of experiences and frame additional inquiries made on descriptions that can guide additional investigation. Allen et al. (2018) states, "We defined reflection as an ongoing, recursive process that practitioners engage in as they deeply analyze the connections between aspects of professional practice. ... This includes instructional planning, teaching, and assessment of learning. We understand products of reflection such as written notes, learning community conversations, and individual commentaries to be momentary windows into practitioners on reflective thinking" (p.83).

It is important for practitioners to recognize that "... reflective practice concerns the self and an understanding of the world. It consists of inquiry into the processes of one's own learning and consideration of one's engagement with teaching and learning. It involves passion, the recognition of intuition and analysis of emotions. It takes the form of a cyclical and continuous process, which requires an ability to negotiate uncertainty" (Swanwick et al., 2014, p. 161). Practicing reflection-on-action allows learners to gradually internalize reflection during the course of action, aiming to develop the skill of reflection-in-action. Schön (1987) refers to this finesse as maneuvering through "... indeterminate zones of practice" (p. 13).

Practitioners can increase their understanding and use of reflective practice by working with colleagues to reflect verbally, using short bursts of information within a conversational environment, formal or casual, or even journaling along with video reflections. Engaging in proactive practice and implementation with formal interactions with team members assists with the creation of an adaptive portfolio of tools in the deployment of reflective practice within multiple everyday settings. Adaptability to differences, expectations, expectations, and environments are key items that practitioners must be able to identify and adjust to in order to use reflective practice effectively.

One of the most used media for developing reflective practice is the reflective journal, since it can provide a venue for learners to develop personally and professionally (Dyment & O'Connell, 2011). Findings indicate that a reflective environment has an incremental effect on students' reflective practices and that reflective practice is dynamic and sensitive to specific learning environment conditions. Reflective learning is based on the circularity between action and reflection, including the practice of questioning our own ways of problem solving. The quality of learning is related to the development of reflective practices, wherein, the professional training approaches pass from the idea of applying theory to the practice of an action-based approach that proposes reflection on the learning activities.

Conversely, conditions that stimulate only cognitive engagement have little impact or even inhibit reflective practices (Bruno & Dell'Aversana, 2018). Assessing the skills of problem-solving, critical thinking and reflective learning are integral to the ultimate aim of transforming classrooms into communities of learning, where students are co-investigators of their own learning. Guided discovery stresses the responsibility that this places on instructors to foster this process in their practice (A. L. Brown, 2009).

Reflective Practice through Experiential Learning Courses

Our classroom and applied experience (via internships and similar field work) can be multidimensional. They can be a source of frustration, excitement, boredom, and even possible alienation. Feelings of loneliness, fear, resentment, envy, and the desire to profit from the misfortunes of others can arise. On the other hand, they can also be an area for fulfillment and meaning for one's life mission and values. Some people learn best with a hands-on approach, dealing directly with the materials that embody or convey the concept. In this way, we also improve the chances that diverse learners with different ways of knowing and differing intelligence profiles can find relevant and engaging ways of learning (Wlodkowski, 2008).

While situated theorizing emphasizes communities as the sites of practice of learning, mainstream accounts of workplace education have also come to emphasize communal facts of learning. It is thus asserted that reflection is more effective – and certainly more critical – when it is a social act (Warhurst, 2008). Using conversation assumptions predicating reflective practice are likely to identify existing practices that are challenging, and then new techniques can be explored. Warhurst (2008) states that "a suitable trajectory of participation is particularly important in facilitating independent reflective learning. Such learning is predicated on newcomers encountering experiences that are comprehensible through their personal reflections" (p. 180). Experiences supportive of practitioners' interaction with colleagues, new situations, and team building activities are rendered meaningful and personal reflective learning.

We learn from experience in numerous ways, through simulated activities, new encounters, or reliving past experiences. Fenwick (2001) notes that practitioners may make sense of their experiences through collaboration with others in a community through introspective experiences such as meditation or dreaming. Courses and activities, including internships and work encounters, are major contributors to gaining experience. However, these experiences cannot happen in a random vacuum of engagements. Instructors and/or supervisors must collaborate to provide structure within the curriculum and employment activities that promote reflective practice. This mode of reflection is also referred to as an embodied mode of reflection, in that it comes about through the physical, lived experience of the practitioner and is revealed through action (Kinsella, 2007).

The classroom or experiential learning site must become living laboratories that promote the use of reflective practice. This can occur using instruction, journaling, simulated meetings, team assignments, along with individual reflection assignments. The use of tacit knowledge is often omitted from the curriculum of reflective practice. However, tacit knowledge is the ordering of the norms and expectations of reality. The ability to be conscious of taking such a stance has implications for practice as it allows practitioners to be freer to test their own theories.

Furthermore, practitioners make tacit knowledge explicit by examining action in practice and by becoming aware of these normative templates that they place on reality. Many practitioners are not mindful of the inherent perspectives they bring to practice and are unconscious of the need to select between them as a point of reference. "This has implications for practice: when practitioners are unaware of their frames for roles or problems, they do not experience the need to choose among them" (Kinsella, 2007, p. 398).

Experience (classroom or internship, etc.) expresses change as a possible outcome within the reflective process. Through reflection one can explore, examine, and censor the tacit know-how learned during their formative years around repetitive experiences of a practice or action(s).

Through reflective practice (in-action, on-action, and for-action), practitioners can make new sense of situations resulting from uncertainty and uniqueness which are experienced in the curriculum, employment, and/or family engagement. In participating in actions or practices that do not work, practitioners have the option of embracing additional theories and practices to make sense of ambiguity and uncertainty.

> **MIRROR MOMENT**
>
> Experiential learning is a cornerstone of reflective practice, leading practitioners to analyze existing practices, beliefs, values, and goals for problems, ineffectiveness, and/or challenges in an effort to determine possible new outcomes. What steps are necessary in outlining an experiential review process using a reflective practice lens?

The use of gaming and simulation within the curriculum enhances opportunities to explore the use of reflective practice in the classroom and can be a precursor for activities and actions within work, community, and family environments. Simulations permit students and instructors to illustrate, discuss, and deploy each phase of reflective practice. As a practice activity, simulations help practitioners in numerous ways, including: collaborating within a learning community; observation of climate and demonstrated culture; suggesting and discussing the possibility of best practices; demonstrating support for possible outcomes; developing skills for the presentation of authentic representation of ideas and concerns; identifying and presenting innovative thinking; and, developing the skills necessary for effective journaling employing what happened today by planning for tomorrow.

Using this skill set to give what it takes to go the extra distance is critical for continuous quality improvement. Simulations and gaming are curriculum aids that provide targeted observations amid collaboration that are meaningful, while exploring elements that can be used to build trusting relationships with colleagues and future co-workers. Brookfield (1987) put it this way: "As people try to make sense of these externally imposed changes, they are frequently at teachable moments as far as becoming critical thinkers ... as people begin to look critically at their past values, common-sense ideas, and habitual behaviors, they begin the precarious business of contemplating new self-images, perspectives, and actions" (p. 11).

FIGURE 9.1 Bridging learning and practice

Reflective practice encourages the use of a process for decision-making. Experience reviewed through a reflective practice lens allows practitioners to seek additional options, check assumptions against reality in making difficult decisions based on beliefs, values, and mission in an effort to determine core priorities. Experience as a process of reflective practice can be an important step toward quality improvement. What the process provides, however, is more inspiring: confidence – not cocky over-confidence that comes from collecting biased information and ignoring uncertainties, but real confidence that comes from knowing you've made the best decision that you could (Heath & Heath, 2013) (Figure 9.1).

Bridging Classroom Learning to Field Practice

Reflective learning, in particular, has now become established as a dominant pedagogy in much of professional development and adult education. Reflective learning must be understood within the social contexts in which it occurs and in the light of differences between individuals and their learning identities (Shamir, 2013). There is no doubt that faculty must find ways to secure the attention of students while providing opportunities for them to focus on learning assignments. All learning contains elements to be grasped/mastered along with communicating cues as to the definition of the elements and how to interact and handle them. The cues can be complex or simple and are often provided in multiple stages during a course or process of instruction. The elements of the instructions may be arranged in several different sequences; there are also instances where they can happen simultaneously.

Faculty provide vital roles in moving students through and within the reflective practice process. The classroom environment becomes a learning laboratory infusing concepts, cues, methods, definitions, and practice into the lives of practitioners. Through their deep reflections within the classroom and assignments, faculty influence learning with lectures, simulations, journaling, digital engagement, and research in an effort to help students capture their experiences for deeper reflections. All of this is accompanied by faculty teaching the use of assessment within reflective practice. We will talk more about assessment in Chapters 12 and 13, but the evaluation process undergirds the importance of understanding reflective learning within a social context that takes place despite differences between individuals and their learning format or style.

Faculty creation of a collaborative environment has the ability to increase students' understanding of professional development and planning. This action over the length of a course or academic program can provide insight into the use of experiential knowledge with colleagues as reflective learning is confirmed and embraced. This provides faculty an opportunity to inclusively develop professional communities within the classroom and beyond, leading to development of a process of nonthreatening, nonevaluative communication. Students benefit when faculty provide a framework for reflective practice that incorporates a high level of instructor effectiveness and efficacy. Through shared reflections with colleagues within their department, faculty can review reflective practice and theory seeking to develop proactive curriculum and activities to encourage student development focused on professional growth beyond their collegiate careers.

> **MIRROR MOMENT**
>
> The transition of knowledge from learning (classroom) to actual engagement (internships or practicums) provides cues to learners on how to prepare and apply skills after completion of an academic course or program of study. What tools can faculty provide to assist students with understanding the use of theory and practice in the workplace that support reflective practice? How can faculty assist students with the deployment of reflective practice during an experiential learning activity, like an internship or practicum? How can faculty plan with career centers and employers to encourage the development and implementation of interactions, evaluation, communication, and the design and implementation of transitional activities to support reflective practice during an experiential learning activity?

Faculty can assist students making the adjustment from the classroom to their professional journey by providing reflective practice that is grounded in professional knowledge and tools through which students learn how to adapt, usage of data to develop informative ideas, possible solutions, and communicate with colleagues and management. Realizing that definitions and terms used to identify reflective practice must be consistent to meet goals of developing student capacities is a vital step between instructors and practitioners. If there is no consistent definition of reflection or common expectation of what reflection should look like in practice, then there is the possibility for ambiguities, confusion, and thus slowing and/or elimination of student progress.

When there is consistency, faculty learn more about their students and are able to develop activities, discussions, simulations, internships, and journaling opportunities to embolden students preparing for new professions. Brookfield (1987) commented that "being a critical thinker is part of what it means to be a developing person, and fostering critical thinking is crucial to creating and maintaining a healthy democracy" (p. 13). Faculty can engage students to demonstrate critical thinking by asking them to reconsider positions discussed during a lecture or discussion – encouraging them to reflect back and consider what they or their colleagues stated to understand the impact of their words and to consider underlying assumptions.

The expression of feelings in reflective practice cannot be overlooked. Although some may consider the expression of feelings in the learning environment to be unusual and out of place, they cannot be ignored. How instructors react can influence how students interpret security and respect. This is a reflective experience students can and will recall during their professional development. How faculty acknowledge and validate feelings is an important component in the reflective learning sequence of events. Ultimately, the goal is to move students to the next-level phase of reflective learning with ideas, concepts, and tools that can provide a degree of confidence.

Cady, Schaak, and Germundsen (2015) describe Reflective Practice Groups as one way faculty can provide a collaborative environment that assists with the development. Students gain insight from conversations and activities supported by their colleagues' experiential backgrounds and knowledge. During the process, community develops as a nonthreatening, nonevaluative setting. A goal of the group process is to unburden practitioners of dilemmas in a supportive environment focused on professional and personal growth.

Creativity in the Reflective Classroom

Although reflective practice is often not intuitive, it is a skill that can be cultivated through development and implementation of a reflective practice curriculum (Saperstein & Seibert, 2015). The curriculum is most effective when it is implemented early (within an academic program of study), and collaboration among the instructional team allows it to continue throughout the course/program of study. An initial step in a reflective practice course is to help students understand the concept of personal context, defined as the interwoven fabric of one's perspective and affective reactions. Embracing this definition enables students to acknowledge that their emotional reactions are neither right nor incorrect; the feelings simply exist. Reflective practice helps us to identify the existence of human reactions, as well as recognize our inability to completely disengage from these feelings.

Through the initial phase of the curriculum, faculty must help students develop an awareness of personal affective reactions and the implications they may have on classmates and future colleagues (not to mention employers). Most of us can recall a situation with a colleague, family member, supervisor, or employer when a situation called for diplomacy or reflection. However, without considering the affective implication of an action or statement that was made, we may not realize why that statement may have derailed a process or projected outcome.

Reflective practice can be fostered by taking an active learning approach, as this provides concrete experiences for individuals and groups to reflect on (N. Brown, 2022). Keeping in mind that students learn through engagement, in addition to gaining experience, they must have time to reflect on what they are doing. Experience and reflection must complement and support one another within the curriculum.

Teaching reflective practice requires time and multiple opportunities for practice as individuals, teams, and groups. After observations, participation, and practice, teams should be asked to reflect together on their experience. Initially, teams should be asked to focus on processes used individually or collectively. The review/discussion should not center on success or failure. Questions similar to the ones below can be used to assist the group with summarization:

- Outline your experience: What happened? What was the end result?
- Impressions and intuitions: What were your feelings before, during and after the engagement?
- Evaluate the engagement (outline both positive and negative). What went well? What did not go so well?
- Analysis (explore the whys): Why did things happen positively? Why was there a negative effect?
- Conclude: What was learned? How could this have been a more positive situation for everyone? What skills do you need to develop to handle a situation like this better?
- Develop an action plan: What would you do differently next time? How would you develop the skills needed? How can you make sure you act differently next time?

Faculty can review and design a plan for discussion with the groups of students about their activity reflections. Summary findings of the encounter can be shared with the entire class. The activity is applicable for each phase of reflective practice: reflection-in-action, reflection-on-action, and reflection-for-action. Reflection on experience is a critical component for learning. Reflective practice, or the capacity to reflect on action and engage in a process of continuous learning, is considered to be a defining characteristic of professional practice (Schön, 1987).

Reflection is not an end in itself, rather a tool or vehicle used in the transformation of raw experience into meaning-field theory that is grounded in experience, informed by existing theory, and serves the larger purpose of the moral growth of individual and society. It is an interactive, forward-moving spiral that moves from practice to theory and theory to practice (Rogers, 2002). The transformational experience of reflective practice requires a social environment in which questioning, thought, synthesis of concepts, and belief in development of practice and progress are possible (Harper, 2018). What is most useful in developing professional expertise through reflective practice is to render tacit knowledge explicit and conscious, thus making it accessible for future use (Schön, 1987).

Case Study

Derrick and Nancy are in their junior year at a state university. The curriculum in the Public Administration program has infused reflective learning into each course. Faculty have worked across the program of study to align curriculum and co-teach sections of courses to ensure congruence in methods, theory, practice, and implementation. The process appeared to meet academic program goals, values, and projected outcomes. Derrick and Nancy worked with the University Career Center to secure internships with a progressive public governmental agency during the first semester of their senior year.

Both students were excited for the opportunity to implement their academic experience in reflective practice. After their orientation and conversations with their supervisors, they realized there was something missing. Each informed their supervisors of their training in reflective practice. The supervisor was amazed and admitted that reflective practice was a foreign concept and never used within the governmental agency. The supervisor, interested in learning more and the possible implementation of reflective practice during internships and beyond, contacted the University Career Center for guidance. They admitted little to no knowledge of reflective practice, suggesting the scheduling of a meeting between the governmental agency, career center, and the public administration faculty.

- As faculty, how would you prepare for this meeting?
- How would you design the agenda?
- What are the possible implications for the program, faculty, students, employer, and career center?
- How would you explain reflective practice and the possible benefits for the agency?
- How would you ensure a continued working relationship with the Career Center using reflective theory and practice?

Conclusion

The human brain retains memories and information. This information is not stored, it is *storied*. The incredible organ we call the brain is a living, dynamic system of neurons and dendrites that retains information in a narrative format. Reflection as preparation embodies the dynamic of the brain's ecosystem. Educators have a goal of developing meaningful, lifelong practices that are supported by continuous learning. Practitioners are challenged with the retention and use of theories and practices associated with common and essential goals they establish as their career focus. These goals are often linked to theories, practices, and challenges that require the use of the brain's ecosystem using reflective practice to cultivate development and implementation of: reflection-in-action, reflection-on-action, and reflection-for-action, fostering an active learning process.

The alignment of theory and practice is often a success indication for practitioners in the public sector, agencies, institutions, and organizations. Often this journey toward understanding the dynamics of intersectionality can lead to low morale. Understanding then leads to application and provides practitioners and leaders with the skills of reflection as a second wind to negotiate the waters enterprises that can be calm and stormy. Next, Chapter 10 will provide navigational insights to perceptions of the public sector.

References

Allen, K. L., Brodeur, K., Israelson, M. H., Martin-Kerr, K.-G., Ortmann, L., & Peterson, D. S. (2018). *Developing reflective practice in teacher candidates through program*. Retrieved from https://creativecommons.org/licenses/by/4.0/

Brookfield, S. D. (1987). *Developing critical thinkers: Challenging adults to explore alternative ways of thinking and acting*. San Francisco, CA: Jossey-Bass.

Brown, A. L. (2009). Design experiments: Theoretical and methodological challenges in creating complex interventions in classroom settings. *Journal of the Learning Sciences, 2*(2), 141–178.

Brown, N. (2022). Teaching reflective practice in teams: In-person and virtual activities. *2022 IEEE Global Engineering Conference*. doi:10.1109/EDUCCON52537.2022.9766457.

Bruno, A., & Dell'Aversana, G. (2018). Reflective practicum in higher education: The influence of the learning environment on the quality of learning. *Assessment & Evaluation in Higher Education, 43*(3), 345–358.

Cady, J. M., Schaak, D., & Germundsen, R. A. (2015). Reflective practice groups in teacher induction: Building professional community via experiential knowledge. *Education, 118*(3), 459–70.

Dyment, J. E., & O'Connell, T. S. (2011). Assessing the quality of reflection in student journals: A review of the research. *Teaching in Higher Education, 16*(1), 89–97.

Fenwick, T. J. (2001). *Experiential learning: A theoretical critique from five perspectives*. Information Series No. 385. ERIC Clearinghouse on Adult, Career and Vocational Education, Center on Education and Training for Employment, Columbus, OH.

Foley, G. (2008). *Dimensions of adult learning: Adult education and training in a global era.* Berkshire, England: Open University Press.

Harper, R. A. (2018). The meaning of doing: Reflective practice in public administration education. *Teaching Public Administration, 36*(2), 143–162.

Heath, C., & Heath, D. (2013). *Decisive how to make better choices in life and work.* New York: Random House.

Kinsella, E. A. (2007). Embodied reflection and the epistemology of reflective practice. *Journal of Philosophy of Education, 41*(3), 395–408.

Rogers, C. R. (2002). Seeing student learning: Teacher change and the role of reflection. *Harvard Educational Review, 72*(2), 230–253.

Saperstein, A. K., & Seibert, D. (2015). A model of teaching reflective practice. *Military Medicine, 180*(4), 142–146.

Schön, D. A. (1987). *Educating the reflective practitioner.* San Francisco, CA: Jossey-Bass.

Shamir, A. (2013). Cognitive education in the digital age: Bridging the gap between theory and practice. *Journal of Cognitive Education and Psychology, 12*(1), 96–107.

Swanwick, R., Kitchen, R., Jarvis, J., McCracken, W., O'Neil, R., & Powers, S. (2014). Following Alice: Theories of critical thinking and reflective practice in action at postgraduate level. *Teaching in Higher Education, 19*(2), 156–169.

Warhurst, R. (2008). Reflections on reflective learning in professional formation. *Studies in the Education of Adults, 40*(2), 176–191.

Wlodkowski, R. J. (2008). *Enhancing adult motivation to learn: A comprehensive guide for teaching all adults third edition.* San Francisco, CA: Jossey-Bass.

10
REFLECTION AS SECOND WIND

Perceptions of the Public Sector

An inside joke among educators goes something like this: "My job would be so much easier if it weren't for students!" We laugh because we recognize how ludicrous the jab is – after all, there would be no need for teachers if it weren't for pupils. It is a symbiotic relationship, just like any other public service profession. Agencies, institutions, and organizations require interactions with the public in order to fulfill their purpose, and the public benefits from the services these entities provide. Nonetheless, the public sector, as a whole, has come under fire in recent years. Nonprofit organizations have fallen into hot water for alleged mismanagement of funds (LeClair, 2019); K-12 educators are under pressure to meet standardized testing expectations with larger class sizes using varied modalities (Deming & Figlio, 2016); higher education institutions are questioned for their worth and impact on society (Oreopoulos & Petronijevic, 2013); governmental agencies are viewed as unnecessarily bureaucratic and corrupt (Ionescu, Lazaroiu, & Iosif, 2012).

Back to the tongue-in-cheek joke, the critique could go multiple ways – some faculty might attest that school administrators actually pile on a heavier burden than students. Any professional throughout the public sector could point to a myriad of stressors that make our jobs frustrating, at times. However, we would be remiss to ignore that the "joke" may be on us, as well. To pose the question pointedly: Those working in public service careers remain under brazen scrutiny by the very populations we serve, yet how do we, in turn, *honestly* view the public? Do public administrators genuinely consider their careers to be a service, or do they harbor resentment toward the public? Researchers refer to this internal perspective toward our work and the

DOI: 10.4324/9781003270775-14

individuals we engage with as *emotional labor*, and it plays an important role in preventing (or exacerbating) burnout (Hsieh, 2014). Throughout this chapter, we will consider morale, participation, and resilience as avenues to incorporate the emotional labor of reflective practice into public sector professions and avoid the burnout trap.

Morale

Even prior to the global health crisis in 2020, many states were already experiencing a K–12 teacher shortage, and since the COVID-19 pandemic, the problem has ballooned – so much so that during the 2021–22 academic year, more than three-quarters of teachers considered leaving their jobs (Marshall, Pressley, Neugebauer, & Shannon, 2022). Faculty are exiting the profession in droves, and those who have stayed report feeling overwhelmed and underappreciated. In an effort to identify risk factors within the teaching profession, one study that explored the reasons for dissatisfaction among public education instructors suggested that "… the principal determinant of burnout is clearly a lack of support and a perception of an inability to control a situation" (Pérez-Luño, Piñol, & Dolan, 2022, p. 780). Teachers are feeling the pressure to do more and more with less and less, yet no end or relief in sight. These notions about support and control are echoed by other studies on the topic of burnout, which we will explore further in this chapter (Figure 10.1).

What is contributing to the loss of morale, not only among educators, but across the public sector, as well? Receiving support from supervisors and/or the organizational system, in general, is a form of extrinsic motivation. This type of morale boost can manifest in countless ways, including tangible perks like casual dress days, swag, and financial bonuses, as well as accolades and other recognition. In terms of intrinsic motivation, this could be classified as perceiving a sense of control over a situation. Each role and individual is different, but maintaining a sense of organization and preparedness can contribute to intrinsic motivation, as might a self-care pep talk that you are good at what you do, and you are doing the best you can. Employers can also support their teams' intrinsic motivation by protecting time for required tasks (rather than expecting staff to take work home – unpaid – after hours) and providing compensated opportunities for training to help sharpen and advance their skills. Both forms of motivation are critically important, in terms of avoiding burnout (Kim, 2018). In their study of public sector professionals' motivations concerning burnout and turnover, Kim also revealed that "… [employers] should increase their intrinsic rather than extrinsic motivation. That is, [employers] should aim to improve their employees' satisfaction with their future possibilities at work, education, and training … all of which would strengthen their pride in their work" (p. 496).

Reflection as Second Wind **127**

> **MIRROR MOMENT**
>
> What do you find pride in, with regard to your professional work? As we implement reflection-in-action, we make adjustments in real time to factors that confront us on the job. What intrinsic and extrinsic factors bring you satisfaction for a job well done?

FIGURE 10.1 More than three-fourth of public school teachers considered quitting in the 2021–2022 academic year

According to the National Library of Medicine within the National Institutes of Health (2020): "There are three main manifestations of symptoms that are considered to be signs of burnout:

- **Exhaustion:** People affected feel drained and emotionally exhausted, unable to cope, tired and down, and don't have enough energy. Physical symptoms include things like pain and gastrointestinal (stomach or bowel) problems.
- **Alienation from (work-related) activities:** People who have burnout find their jobs increasingly stressful and frustrating. They may start being cynical about their working conditions and their colleagues. At the same time, they may increasingly distance themselves emotionally, and start feeling numb about their work.
- **Reduced performance:** Burnout mainly affects everyday tasks at work, at home or when caring for family members. People with burnout are very negative about their tasks, find it hard to concentrate, are listless and lack creativity."

A study by Vella and McIver (2019) identified emotional exhaustion as the first recognizable phase of burnout, which echoes the National Library of Medicine's overview of the issue. The educators' joke mentioned at the beginning of the chapter also ties in with the Alienation indicator mentioned above. When we get to the point of being calloused or snarky about our day-to-day work, that is a red flag that there could be an undercurrent of burnout developing. If we recognize these trigger points and become aware of how prevalent they are, then we can learn to combat them as they occur.

The National Library of Medicine's definition of burnout provides us with a prime example of all three reflective practice stages: reflection-on-action, which refers to consideration of past experiences; reflection-in-action (making adjustments in real time); and reflection-for-action, that is, using reflective practice to manage expectations and plan future goals. *Exhaustion* is an indicator that experiences to date have resulted in mental and physical fatigue (reflection-on-action). *Alienation*, as noted previously, suggests that our work in the moment is negatively affected (reflection-in-action). *Reduced Performance* factors in as a trigger point to make improvements for future behavior or goals (reflection-for-action).

Appreciative Inquiry

A study by O'Brien on morale and job satisfaction among government agency employees, in particular, referenced a line of research called appreciative inquiry, which hinges on identifying affirming aspects of a situation, rather than merely focusing on problems (O'Brien, 2002). We discussed another angle of this approach in Chapter 8 with regard to the Strengths Perspective. In a nutshell, "... appreciative inquiry empowers practitioners to become change agents and to explore innovative practice" (Hung et al., 2018, p. 2). We introduced the Kolb learning cycle briefly in Chapter 1 and will delve into it further in Chapter 12, but there are interesting overlaps between Kolb's perspective on experiential learning and the appreciative inquiry model for practitioners.

The appreciative inquiry framework, as noted by O'Brien (2002), involves four stages: discovery, dream, design, and delivery (p. 31). There are also four steps of the Kolb cycle: Experience, Reflection, Thinking, and Acting. The discovery phase of appreciative inquiry encourages participants to consider positive scenarios and *experiences* from within the organization. The dream step invites brainstorming (or *reflection*) about what the organization might look like at its peak performance. Design is an opportunity to *think* and plan about the organization's future, and delivery is the *action* step to put the plan into motion.

While cultivating an awareness of burnout is important regardless of one's profession, our focus here is primarily on those with careers in public service. In a study of psychosocial hazards on the job, Liu and Cheng (2018) found that public sector professionals faced heightened risks of workplace violence and burnout, compared to peers employed in the private sector.

MIRROR MOMENT

Identify some of the psychosocial hazards affiliated with your line of work (whether you have experienced them personally or not). Using the definition of burnout and reflective stages mentioned above, how might you prepare to combat these risks on the job?

Participation and Power Dynamics

As we shift gears to consider the role of empowerment – both introspectively within ourselves as public service professionals, as well as throughout our interactions with clients, students, etc., it is important to remember that, "what [practitioners] are doing is not to work *for* service users but to work *with* them" (Kam, 2021, p. 1441). With a Strengths Perspective in mind, Kam noted that having an awareness of others' abilities and positive contributions "... also helps to deconstruct [employees'] negative image of disadvantaged service users" (p. 1427). This rationale dovetails with the critique mentioned at the beginning of the chapter about how burnout can manifest as job dissatisfaction and even sarcasm toward the public, in general.

We discussed the Strengths Perspective in much more detail in Chapter 8, but it is important to make the connection again here with regard to empowerment as a defense against burnout. Being mindful of our strengths helps us to shift the focus from simply problem-solving to finding motivation for improvement. We know rationally that we, as well as our clients, students, colleagues, and customers have inherent strengths, but what steps can we take to recognize those attributes, so we can empower them to use and grow those strengths? Kam (2021) outlined ten ways of identifying service users' strengths:

1. Look for other possibilities beyond the obvious. If someone is routinely punctual, for example, it might also stand to reason that they have pretty strong organizational skills, given their time management precedent.
2. Rather than focusing on problems, coach them to brainstorm their interests. How someone spends their free time might be an indicator of their natural inclinations and strong suits.
3. The here and now is important, but also be cognizant of someone's past experiences as examples of ways they have overcome challenges.
4. What stands out as unique? Keep an eye out for strength areas that you might not expect to see.
5. Don't box anyone in. An academic might have a hobby as a shade tree mechanic. Conversely, a blue-collar worker could be very well read. Don't allow stereotypes within social constructs to inhibit your openness to others' strengths.
6. Consider someone's strengths in varied contexts. How do their strengths suit their present role(s)? What other roles might they thrive in?
7. Strengths may also point us to our areas of improvement. Someone who is extremely driven, for example, may also struggle with setting unrealistic expectations.
8. Encourage opportunities for individuals to branch out and try something new, to engage in experiences that stretch their comfort zones.
9. Recognize that sometimes, we discover our strengths through adversity because we have to find ways to cope.
10. Don't forget external influences like family relationships and membership in groups or community organizations as potential contributors to one's strengths.

The aforementioned O'Brien (2002) study also identified four key themes to aid public administrators in their efforts to avoid burnout: self-care, relationships, learning opportunities, and feeling valued. *Self-care* and *feeling valued* go hand-in-hand as intrinsically powerful motivators, in that they both hinge on an inside-out focus on ourselves. In this particular study, *self-care* includes personal perceptions such as confidence and optimism, while *feeling valued* has to do with traits like trustworthiness and whether someone feels like they are making a difference. By contrast, *relationships* and *learning opportunities* are extrinsic; they rely on others' input to manifest. The *relationships* component deals with feelings of belongingness, connection, and teamwork, whereas *learning opportunities* come to light with innovation and new challenges. Interestingly, although the study parceled out *feeling valued* into its own criterion, the concept of individual value also rose to the top of the three other categories. One might interpret the findings to say that we, as public administrators, have a deeply seated need to know not only that we have an impact on a personal level, but also that our investment matters to the organization and people we serve.

Speaking of impact on multiple fronts, Kam (2021) recommended that social work practitioners develop an Empowerment-Participation-Strengths Model when interacting with their clients. Elements of this model have already been addressed above, in terms of identifying service users' strengths. The model also highlighted three key levels of empowerment, which we will unpack here and begin to draw broader applications beyond a therapy setting. The first empowerment level is *personal*, with a focus on our individual competence and impact on the work of the organization. This phase ties in with what we have learned about ourselves using the Strengths Perspective. When we're aware of the skills we possess, we feel more empowered to contribute through active participation. That confidence then feeds our ability to move to the next level of empowerment.

Second, we explore the *interpersonal* level, particularly with regard to reducing or eliminating negative stereotypes within society. We touched on this topic briefly earlier when discussing the think-outside-the-box strategy concerning service users' strengths. Another way we can help advocate against – and, ultimately, eliminate – prejudices is to amplify the voices of the underrepresented and marginalized. A silent supporter is not particularly effective when a contentious topic is on the agenda. Being an advocate means leveraging our privilege, even (perhaps *especially*) in the workplace. This is the heart of reflection-for-action, because we can make a positive impact on future scenarios that we have yet to encounter. Professional athlete and author, Abby Wambach (2019), summarized the call to action this way:

> If you have a voice, you have influence to spread.
> If you have relationships, you have hearts to guide.
> If you know young people, you have futures to mold.
> If you have privilege, you have power to share.
> If you have money, you have support to give.
> If you have a ballot, you have policy to shape.
> If you have pain, you have empathy to offer.
> If you have freedom, you have others to fight for.
> If you are alive, you are a leader.
> *p. 42*

Finally, we examine *structural* empowerment, in the sense of acting in unison to hash out problems and face social inequalities and injustice head-on. Think about the organizational structure at your workplace. As we navigate our way through these three levels of empowerment, we start with ourselves – that introspective place where we focus on the workings of our own minds and the skills and strengths that we possess. As we grow and develop that level, we have influence over our interpersonal relationships, which is the second step of empowerment. Here, we collaborate with our colleagues, teams, and small groups. Structural empowerment takes place when the interpersonal empowerment we have cultivated begins to affect positive change within the organization. Here, we might see changes to the strategic plan and goals – even the organization's mission statement, which reflect these systemic adjustments.

In order for the process to be effective, our efforts must engage those we are seeking to empower. Kam (2021) refers to this as the "ladder of service user participation" (p. 1434), though we will consider applications to the public sector workforce, at large.

- Being consulted/giving feedback: In higher education, this feedback loop often takes place in the context of what is known as *shared governance*. Ideally, shared governance represents multiple voices throughout the decision-making process, including not only administration but also faculty, staff, and students. In the nonprofit sector, it might look like engaging board members with staff and donors. Regardless of the method for soliciting feedback, it is important that stakeholders have the opportunity to weigh in and offer their insights.
- Being offered more opportunities to make choices: Within the public sector, this type of input might materialize as focus groups. For example, consider a public library to which a benefactor has donated several million dollars through their estate planning bequest. The library might seek out connections with staff, patrons, area schools, community leaders, and local or regional government officials to solicit input about the needs and wish lists for various stakeholders to improve the library's physical space, digital offerings, and in-person activities.
- Being involved in daily service management and implementation: Consider inviting alumni, clients, board members, volunteers, and other stakeholders to share their personal experiences with the organization during board meetings, donor galas, alumni gatherings, and community events. Not only does this approach engage these key individuals in a way that may help them to feel more deeply invested in the organization, but sharing stories is also a common strategy in fundraising circles to generate greater affinity toward the organization.
- Assist in running programs/community activities: Rather than just having staff plan the annual 5K Fun Run fundraiser, why not solicit involvement

of volunteers and participants who have utilized the organization's programs and services? This helps to put a face to the work of the organization and is an impactful way to share success stories with potential donors and other prospective stakeholders.
- Active participation in groups/community projects: This suggestion dovetails with the one just prior, but the twist is for the organization to actively seek input from stakeholders with regard to future planning. Perhaps a nonprofit organization or local government service agency would be open to hosting a booth at a county fair or downtown street festival, and the individuals volunteering at the table could include participants and/or alumni, rather than just staff or board members.
- Partnership: The shared governance example, above, is one example of formal partnerships. Advisory groups comprised of community members, donors, and other advocates are another option for public sector entities to build strong ties within their local communities and beyond to further the goals of the organization.
- Decision-making and control: Rather than pad the Board of Directors with high rollers in the community, an organization might consider inviting actual stakeholders to participate at this important level of decision-making. One example of this strategy done well is Independent Living organizations,[1] which serve individuals with disabilities to help them remain as independent as feasible for as long as possible. Some of these county- or regionally focused organizations have a mandate in their bylaws to have at least half of the board members be people with disabilities. This approach helps to ensure that the organization remains mindful of their clientele and keeps their mission as the focal point of all decision-making.

Case Study

A 5th grade teacher with 16 years' experience in the classroom shared her candid perspective on burnout in a public service profession:

> I know what I allegedly *should* do to not get swamped and feel burned out, while still leaving the school building in a timely manner so I can actually spend time with family and do some self-care. The right thing to do is set myself daily and weekly to-do lists, so I don't feel overwhelmed with routine things like lesson plans, making copies, and communicating with parents. Instead, what ends up happening is that the workload continues to grow without extra time or pay to get it all done, so the to-dos build up and build up. Additional tasks that the administration says are only supposed to take a few minutes apiece actually end up taking four more hours, collectively.

It doesn't end, and it's a lot. What I do is work 12–13 hour days, come home and have a late dinner, then work 2–4 more hours each night. The weekend is also mostly work. So, when I'm facing that and it's overwhelming and I'm feeling burned out, I know I need to step back, reassess my time, and prioritize what has to be done that day. I have to give tasks time deadlines to make myself go home. But then, tasks build up and become a cyclical stress cycle that doesn't end until the summer.

I had four days this week where I was at work until 7:00 p.m. I'm there before 7:00 a.m. every day. There's traffic on the way home. I eat dinner, then work more until past bedtime. Night before last, I was sending email at 11:30pm, because it had to get done. I also have a mentee that I have to train that is only supposed to take a half-hour a week, but that isn't realistic with all the expectations and pressure of that role. And that's not even including all the parents I have to talk to, staff meetings, special education accommodations, and disciplinary situations with students.

The district expects us to have stations within the classroom, geared toward individual levels. I have 24 students in the class, so I put them into groups of three, which results in multiple versions of the same lessons and all the extra workload that comes with grading each of those different assignments. The irony is that the state standardized exam isn't based on levels, so I spend hours planning individualized lessons, but it looks like nothing in the end.

I'm set up for failure, no matter what I do or how hard I work, I will never achieve all the tasks that are assigned to me. I'm not paid for all these hours. The worst is when I finally just mentally check out. I hit a brick wall and just quit. In those moments, I know that I'll pay for it in even more deadlines and stress later, but right then, I just can't do another thing.

If you're able to teach past 3–5 years – those are the big exodus years. At that point, you aren't doing it for the money; you're doing it for the kids. You're doing it for the a-ha moment of their understanding, that spark. It makes you feel good. I can't leave now because I feel pigeonholed. I'm at an age where I don't know what else I would do with my degree and experience.

Besides, I can't afford to miss a paycheck, and I'm under a yearly contract. If I break my contract, then I lose my teaching certificate. If I leave in the middle of the school year, my teaching certificate will be revoked. You sign a contract for the following year before the current year is even over. There's only about a 6-week window to find another job. Honestly, there's also a fear of the unknown: even though the present situation is overwhelming, I know what to do. Leaving for another job means that teaching couldn't be a fall-back, because my certificate would be revoked. So, I'm stuck.

It stands to reason that the primary motivation for public school teachers to stay in the profession is intrinsic, such as the "a-ha moment" that our case study mentions. Most public school teachers (at least in the United States) are not extrinsically motivated by having a competitive salary. In fact, in 2020–21, the average annual salary of teachers in public elementary and secondary schools in the U.S. was roughly $65,000, with some states averaging only in the upper-40s (National Center for Education Statistics, 2021). To put this range into context, a public school teacher in the U.S. makes slightly more than an average bar manager (Talent.com, 2022), and roughly as much or even less than a Specialty Area Manager at Walmart, such as the produce department lead or head of asset management (Walmart, 2022). If extrinsic motivation is not a consideration, then given the personal, interpersonal, and structural stages of empowerment, what would you recommend for our teacher to try to implement in order to improve her situation?

Considering further what you have read about power dynamics and participation, how might you advise principals, superintendents, school board members, parents and other community members, as well as state-level policy makers about improving the morale of school teachers? Should we invest more, as a collective, to better support public school teachers? Why or why not? If the answer is yes, then where do we begin?

Conclusion

As we wrap up this chapter on reflective practice as a tool to ward off burnout, one takeaway is that burnout is not simply an individual experience. We saw in the example of the public school teacher that unrealistic expectations of a particular job and the high pressure environment also play an important role in perpetuating feelings of burnout. In the next chapter, we will explore organizational culture in more detail to see how we can implement reflective practice to help guide and improve the workplace, collectively.

Note

1 An example of an Independent Living organization with this board membership protocol is RRCI, headquartered in Southern Utah: www.rrci.org

References

Deming, D. J., & Figlio, D. (2016). Accountability in US education: Applying lessons from k-12 experience to higher education. *Journal of Economic Perspectives*, *30*(3), 33–56.

Hsieh, C.-W. (2014). Burnout among public service workers. *Review of Public Personnel Administration*, *34*(4), 379–402.

Hung, L., Phinney, A., Chaudhury, H., Rodney, P., Tabamo, J., & Bohl, D. (2018). Appreciative inquiry. *International Journal of Qualitative Methods, 17*(1), 160940691876944.

Ionescu, L., Lazaroiu, G., & Iosif, G. (2012). Corruption and bureaucracy in public services. *Amfiteatru Economic, 14*(Special Issue 6), 665–679.

Kam, P. K. (2021). From the strengths perspective to an empowerment-participation-strengths model in social work practice. *British Journal of Social Work, 51*, 1441.

Kim, J. (2018). The contrary effects of intrinsic and extrinsic motivations on burnout and turnover intention in the public sector. *International Journal of Manpower, 39*(3), 486–500.

LeClair, M. S. (2019). Malfeasance in the charitable sector: Determinants of "Soft" corruption at nonprofit organizations. *Public Integrity, 21*(1), 54–68. doi:10.1080/10999922.2017.1422310.

Liu, H.-C., & Cheng, Y. (2018). Psychosocial work hazards, self-rated health and burnout: A comparison study of public and private sector employees. *Journal of Occupational and Environmental Medicine, 60*(4), E193–E198.

Marshall, D. T., Pressley, T., Neugebauer, N. M., & Shannon, D. M. (2022). Why teachers are leaving and what we can do about it. *Phi Delta Kappan, 104*(1), 6–11.

National Center for Education Statistics. (2021, August). *Digest of Education Statistics: Estimated average annual salary of teachers in public elementary and secondary schools, by state: Selected years, 1969–70 through 2020–21.* Retrieved from https://nces.ed.gov/programs/digest/d21/tables/dt21_211.60.asp

National Library of Medicine. (2020, June 18). *Depression: What is burnout?* Retrieved from https://www.ncbi.nlm.nih.gov/books/NBK279286/

O'Brien, R. F. (2002). *Job satisfaction and morale in public service: An appreciative approach within the ministry of children and family development* (Order No. MQ70934). ABI/INFORM Collection; ProQuest Dissertations & Theses Global (305481622). Retrieved from https://www.proquest.com/dissertations-theses/job-satisfaction-morale-public-service/docview/305481622/se-2

Oreopoulos, P., & Petronijevic, U. (2013). Making college worth it: A review of the returns to higher education. *The Future of Children, 23*(1), 41–65.

Pérez-Luño, A., Piñol, M. D., & Dolan, S. L. (2022). Exploring high vs. low burnout amongst public sector educators: COVID-19 antecedents and profiles. *International Journal of Environmental Research and Public Health, 19*(2), 780. doi:10.3390/ijerph19020780.

Talent.com. (2022). *Bar manager salary in the USA, 2022.* Retrieved from https://www.talent.com/salary?job=bar±manager

Vella, E., & McIver, S. (2019). Reducing stress and burnout in the public-sector work environment: A mindfulness meditation pilot study. *Health Promotion Journal of Australia, 30*(2), 219–227.

Walmart. (2022). *Walmart store management jobs.* Retrieved from https://careers.walmart.com/stores-clubs/walmart-management-jobs#:~:text=You%20may%20be%20surprised%20to,of%20%2450%2C000%20to%20%24170%2C000%20annually

Wambach, A. (2019). *WOLFPACK: How to come together, unleash our power, and change the game.* New York: Little, Brown Book Group.

PART IV
Reflection for Organizational Change

11
REFLECTION AS CULTURE

A culture of reflection is an important part of the learning process for leaders and practitioners in both formal and informal learning environments. Reflection is an action(s) that is considered persistent and careful consideration is given to beliefs, values, and practices or supposed forms of knowledge in reference to the process and procedures that support it and the conclusions to which it leads (Dewey, 1916). Dewey supported the need for a method of learning based on the examination of a person's experience and the various environments associated with learning. This introspection is but one aspect of reflective practice, and as we will see in this chapter, it goes well beyond individual use and can be influential at the organizational level, as well.

Reflection in a classroom environment permits students to compare and contrast the paths, markers, and maps each uses to find answers while providing a vessel for students to interact with the instructor and each other through questions, answers, and sharing ideas in the traditional classroom setting or alternative modes of instructional delivery such as distance or hybrid modalities. Done effectively, spontaneous reflective thinking must have at its heart a commitment to action and deliberate critical thinking (White, 2008). This chapter identifies the key elements needed in the creation and deployment of a reflective culture, with a focus on how teacher/student and peer/peer interactions are enhanced by the various methods of instruction used to champion learning in a cultural environment that encourages reflective practice.

What Is a Culture of Reflective Practice?

A culture of reflective practice is evident in an organization that embraces reflective growth as a primary driving force behind the continuous, lasting improvement. Within the organization, members speak the language of reflection, engage in rigorous metacognitive tasks, and earnestly support their individual and collective growth (Hall & Simeral, 2017). Metacognition pertains to thinking about the way one thinks. Reflection, more specifically, is a way of thinking about actions and responses using existing and newly gained knowledge. In a nutshell, reflection is learning from experience by considering what one knows, believes, and values within the context of current situations and then reframing to develop future decision-making. Thus, reflective practice is essentially an extension of evidence-based practices and research (Sherwood & Horton-Deutsch, 2015). This focus forms the foundation of building a culture of reflective practice.

It is important to remember that organizational culture can be difficult to define due to their complexity, yet every organization has a distinctive and identified culture, consisting of values, customs, and beliefs that configure behaviors and relationships. Organizational theories can help to illuminate and understand culture by explaining concepts and enhancing cultural elements important to the organization and its mission. From these foundational points, the organization can begin to identify enhanced and dysfunctional patterns that help in the understanding of the organization's current culture and the need for transformation and change. Schein (1992) conceived of culture existing at three levels:

- Artifacts, which include iconic architecture, lore, and traditions.
- Values, including the makeup of governing bodies and their rationale for policies and actions.
- Organizational culture, which encompasses the underlying assumptions of the organization's values. Articulated values, much like mission and vision statements, do not guide our understanding about why an organization functions the way it does. Values alone do not and cannot explain the driving force or essence of culture. Much like the definition of metacognition at an individual level as thinking about the way one thinks, an organization's overarching culture is created by how people reflect upon the values within the organization.

Reflective culture can be shaped by how work is accomplished and how problems are resolved. The assumptions of and about an organization's culture shape and deploy employees' thoughts, perceptions, feelings, and behaviors, assisting in guiding an institution's relationship with community stakeholders, and the nature of internal and external relationships. Culture and continuous quality improvements are contingent on cultural adjustment and change.

Consequently, change is a fundamental process dependent upon experience and knowledge acquired. Therefore, a culture of reflective practice is developed as a learning process examining current and past experiences, behaviors, and thoughts to make choices about future actions that can improve the organization. A reflective culture is not a one-off process. It is a living institutional organism that uses experience, knowledge, research, and foresight to continuously encourage communications, and actions to grow and develop organizations, communities, and stakeholders (both internal and external).

> **MIRROR MOMENT**
>
> Reflective culture embraces growth as a foundational cornerstone for an organization's continuous improvement. To support the improvement, member organizations engage in metacognitive tasks (thinking about the ways in which we think). How would you use metacognition within the development of a reflective practice culture in your own team, institution, or organization?

Why a Reflective Culture?

Cultivating a culture of reflexive practice provides an institution with the ability to address current and future challenges with an ongoing series of communication, formats, and skills to encourage forward thinking. A reflective culture can only occur by moving beyond present-day issues, problems, and ideas. Challenges that an institution faces currently can present a unique opportunity to address the immediate concern and build operational activities, values, and plans for future adaption of new standards that move the organization forward proactively. Moving toward a reflective culture is not an overnight process. Reflective practice is the common thread among transformative organizations, like we explored in Chapter 4.

As group members in the organization act reflectively on experience and reframe old patterns into new processes and workflows, they help to create a reflective organization focused on continuous learning and improvement. The reflective cultural journey begins with effective change, which is a complicated process that involves a series of steps:

- Focus on clear purpose of the desired change
- Manage challenges
- Sustain change
- Use reflective assessment and evaluation of change to tell the story of managing the complexities of change and transformation

Change for change's sake is often met with resistance, such as a new vice president joining an organization and immediately restructuring the organizational chart. Without a clear purpose, the change can be interpreted by the team as undesirable and unnecessary. Change is inherently important in order for an organization to continue to grow, adapt, and thrive, but the purpose of and rationale for the changes need to be clearly communicated.

A reflective administrator will also effectively manage challenges that arise along the way and design scaffolding within the organization to sustain the changes over time. The reflective cultural journey can help organizations examine how to shift from being a static, traditionally minded organization into a transformative, reflective learning entity focused on continuous improvement. The goal of this journey is to help change-seekers with an integration of new competencies and concepts that the organization can use to address necessary adjustments by sharing stories (focusing on the clear purpose) and incorporating reflective practice.

Communication is an essential organizational process and shapes culture; culture and communication are interwoven, such that culture is lived through the interactions of its members (Bellot, 2011). Ongoing communication with and among team members leads to interpretations and evaluation by the organization using a number of approaches. Organizations are improved and sustained through the way culture manages the change processes, shares stories, resolves problems and conflict, and approaches teaching and learning (Singer et al., 2009).

Shared mental models are the overlapping concepts held by group members and include the thought processes about how something works in the real world. These shared explanations serve to get everyone on the same page and lessen the ambiguity about organizational culture through common representations of events and concepts. Shared mental models provide a framework to assess and explain what happens in the organizational environment. Organizations are in the business of knowledge management and supporting knowledge workers; therefore, the act of reflective practice becomes a key business strategy. It encourages workers to reflect in meaningful ways on what is and isn't working in the organization. It also provides a natural structure for mentoring and peer feedback as employees work together to solve individual and collective problems and find solutions to nagging questions (Martin, n.d.).

At the center of reflective practice is an inquiry to ask why is this happening and what can we do about it? Questioning is important to both individual and organizational improvement, much like we discussed in Chapter 7 regarding doubt. Absent from questioning, efforts are stagnated, and change becomes less meaningful. Reflective questioning is a powerful way for practitioners to examine their current performance, consequences of their actions, and future possibilities. A collaborative culture of inquiry can be encouraged through using reflective questioning strategies and collaborative improvement initiatives such as visioning, action research, and professional development. Reflective practice helps identify opportunities for growth and skill attainment. It helps organizations identify knowledge gaps and skill shortages. Pockets of innovation, creativity, and mastery performance are also discovered.

While a progressively focused culture of inquiry can be valuable to an organization, questioning without a framework or guide to the conversation can devolve into complaining, bickering, and infighting. Wolfberg and Dixon (2011) remind us that organizations must be careful not to support counter-productive points that defeat reflective culture:

- Asserting one's own views without revealing the reason behind them
- Discouraging inquiry into their reasoning
- Minimizing or avoiding any inquiry into another person's point of view
- Asking leading questions to convince others their own point of view is the correct one
- Responding and acting on untested assumptions (usually negative about motives behind the other person's actions).

Earlier in this section, the term action research was used as a possible tool to support improvement initiatives. Action research is a participatory, democratic process concerned with developing practical knowing in the pursuit of worthwhile human purposes, grounded in a participatory worldview. It seeks to bring together action and reflection, theory and practice, in participation with others, in the pursuit of practical solutions to issues of pressing concern to people (Reason & Bradbury, 2001). This form of research can be performed immediately without an extreme production or elaborate preparation. Niculescu (2014) describes it as a process for investigating not only social and political conditions but also for work and learning. Action research used in support of reflective practice enables conceiving of and achieving strategies that can aid an organization in addressing complexities and uncertainties that arise while building a reflective and forward-thinking culture.

> **MIRROR MOMENT**
>
> Action research is considered to be a form of research that embraces direct engagement with participants of a group to improve the quality of the community studied. How would you use action research to assist and deploy strategies approved in a reflection-for-action problem-solving sessions within a team you are leading?

Key Elements in Creating a Culture of Reflection

Establishing a reflective culture requires organizations to develop climates that support each phase of reflective practice: reflection-in-action, reflection-on-action, and reflection-for-action. Leaders must be dedicated to active learning.

144 Reflection for Organizational Change

FIGURE 11.1 Creating a culture of reflection

Active learning seeks to involve the learner beyond the formal classroom. Its purpose is to develop professional capability for practitioners. Courses and professional interactions are informed and designed by learning outcomes practitioners are expected to achieve, which in turn are informed by conceptions of competence and capability. How leaders think about capable professionals is the higher order premise – implicitly or explicitly – that drives teaching and professional development efforts. Reflective practice seeks to develop practitioners who are more than simply being competent in designated tasks and the routine application of previously acquired knowledge and skill (Lizzio & Wilson, 2004) (Figure 11.1).

The higher order notion of adaptive flexibility builds upon the idea of simply being capable. Through field studies on the functioning of senior managers, Klemp and McClelland (1986) identified the construct of adaptation as the key to leaders' success. Adaptability, in this sense, is seen as having the capacity to enact specific combinations of competencies in appropriate context.

Faculty and other leaders must establish learning environments that support authentic tasks that are appropriate and relevant to the learning styles of each student. Reflective culture must provide access to learning tools, technology, and developmental environments that are effective.

Implementing active learning environments that focus on practitioners independent and collective learning that is different from traditional face-to-face sessions. Such engagements must encourage a transfer of knowledge, problem-solving, understanding, utilization of applications, individual and group work, discussion, and consensus building (Yajima, Yoshihiro, Sato, Ichimura, & Kishimoto, 2022). Educators must be clear and open to feedback while encouraging collaborative dialogues between teachers/students and between peers. Hall and Simeral (2017) contend that constant and regular communication, a dedication to the goals of a culture of reflective practice, and a consistent level of intentionality in the use of reflective language, the implementation of a culture of reflective practice can remain at the forefront of the organization.

Leadership is an essential component of cultural development. Leaders at all levels (from the frontlines, classroom, and boardroom) must display competencies that build and support a culture of reflective practice. The following are questions to consider:

- What are the levels and knowledge, skills, and capabilities leaders need to forge and maintain an organizational commitment that will produce reflective practitioners of the future?
- How do current institutional policies support change management for cultural adjustment/development, innovation, and action in developing a desired future?
- What are the leadership competencies that support the creation of innovative cultural change?
- How does one exercise leadership influence to build a culture of reflective practice?

The transformation to a culture of reflective practice requires visionary thinking, energizing, and stimulating change processes that engage people and communities in the design and development of a new model (Sherwood & Horton-Deutsch, 2015).

The environment must be safe and nonthreatening, allowing teachers/facilitators to model images students/practitioners can mirror. Reflective learning mirrors phases of critical thinking, beginning with a trigger event – an unexpected experience causing a sense of inner discomfort. Next comes appraisal, or scrutinizing situations that follow the trigger event. Exploration occurs when individuals recognize anomalies or discrepancies in some aspect of life and begin to search for new ways of explaining or coming to terms with these issues in ways that reduce our sense of discomfort. Developing alternative perspectives arises out of the testing and exploring of alternatives come ways of thinking that we feel make sense for our situations. Lastly, integration takes place when we have decided on the worth, accuracy, and validity of new ways of thinking or living and begin to find ways to fold these concepts into the fabric of our lives (Brookfield, 1987).

Harkness, Porter, and Hettich (2001) explain that by using the five teaching methods of modeling, coaching, scaffolding, reflection, and articulation, the teacher/facilitator can guide the learner down the path of becoming an expert by providing opportunities to succeed based on the individual need or previous experiences of the learner. One way to do this could be establishing journals, discussion boards, and learning communities that support the sharing of information while providing the teacher/facilitators with valuable insights into group and individual reflections.

Reflective culture encourages learners to move beyond elementary analysis of experience. Through reflective action, learners review the actual process of how they execute acting, feeling, and thinking. The various modes of a reflective culture explore the how, what, and why questions in solving a problem during a review of a prior experience. Developing habits of continual growth and improvement requires self-reflection. As individuals, teams, and larger organizations reflect on our actions, we gain important information about the efficacy of our thinking. These experiences let us practice the habit of continual growth through reflection. Costa and Kallick (2000) explain that with meditation, trust, consistent modeling, and practice, we and our students/ practitioners learn to listen to the internal and external voices of reflection and in the process our communities truly learn by doing.

A culture of reflective practice is collective (building collective capacity) and differentiated (building individual capacity). Organizations are no longer isolated by profession. Individuals, teams, divisional, and department units cannot ignore the collective knowledge and experience colleagues and peers offer. Leaders and colleagues must encourage all to rise to the challenge. This is the nature of collaboration and in a culture of reflective practice, growth and change are a part of the collective future.

> **MIRROR MOMENT**
>
> Administrators are given the task of articulating the vision of our developing culture of reflective practice to faculty, staff, students, and the institution's stakeholders. The organization's leadership team is aligned and determined reflective culture to be a real practice. They want all employees to embrace reflective practice individually, as well as engage in reflection with each other throughout the organization.

- How do you communicate this expectation?
- Outline the variety of ways you would use to engage staff.
- What are your first three steps? How will you use reflective practice to move this assignment forward?

Language as Culture

Language is an essential part of building relationships within communities. Language allows for the sharing of words, thoughts and ideas as a primary form of communication. It is widely believed that there is a natural connection between the language spoken by members of a social group and that group's identity. By their accent, their vocabulary, and their discourse patterns, speakers identify themselves and are recognized as members of this or that speech and discourse community. Kramsch (1998) noted that from this membership, they draw personal strength and pride, as well as a sense of social importance and historical continuity from using the same language as the group they belong to (p. 65). Cross-cultural engagement within education, work, family, and community is important to the unique development and growth of an organization. Language reflects culture and can demonstrate nationality and regional dialects.

There are challenges that exist when different languages are used within cross-cultural communities and the barriers can influence the bond created with social, political, and work environments. Language and culture have an imminent role in bringing together economic, political, and community stakeholders. Language is more than just words to convey communication; it has personal and cultural relevance, and the power to engage emotions along with an array of meanings. How one uses words, phrases, and gestures conveys a lot about them.

Reflective practice provides an opportunity to explore cross-cultural language identities among practitioners within work, community, and educational environments. Groups and teams can engage in reflection-in-action, reflection-on-action, and reflection-for-action to share lifestyles, values, and social differences in an effort to understand and build an organizational connection. Reflective practice can assist leaders in establishing such connections that contribute to the creation of a common organizational language that provides a sense of ownership and belonging with the values, beliefs, and principles of an organization.

Case Study

A large nonprofit organization has determined, using the results of a culture and climate study survey, that their existing culture is not meeting the needs of its community stakeholders and workforce. The organization is eager to engage in a series of informal lunch discussions, listening sessions, and appreciative inquiry meetings to determine the direction for cultural change. The leadership team and board of directors understand that knowledge, choice, perception, and prior experience are several of the key elements that will be used to evaluate their level of leadership and organizational performance.

The organizational leadership turns to you and other administrators to lead the process toward cultural change. During a meeting with your team, the Chief Executive Officer and board members express interest in the exploration of a reflective practice culture. Your team agrees to review and share with the organization for feedback.

Using each of the reflective practice steps (reflection-in-action, reflection-on-action, and reflection-for-action), what process (steps) will you use to engage organizational employees and community stakeholders in addressing the following questions?

- How does our current culture support innovation and action to service our community into the future?
- What are the leadership competencies that can support the development of an innovative organizational culture?
- How does one exercise leadership influence to build an organizational culture that is future-focused?

Sherwood and Horton-Deutsch (2015) suggest that building a culture of reflective practice has measurable consequences. The return on investment for organizations can be significant and may be the difference between surviving in a competitive landscape or losing enrollment or going out of business. Organizational culture can be extremely difficult to understand and analyze; however, it is critical to improving the services such as teaching and learning. The use of experiential and transformational theories assists with the engagement of practitioners in new activities where they are able to test ideas, make applications, and evaluate the implication for future activities. Through reflecting on experiences together, leaders and practitioners learn how to assimilate and transform abstract concepts into new ideas for addressing change (Sherwood & Horton-Deutsch, 2015).

Reflection is a skill that can be developed and cultivated. Practitioners are unique and each may approach reflective practice differently; thus, they require tools to assess how practitioners reflect (their cognitive process) and to align the kind of support and tools each practitioner that is compatible with their learning needs. If leaders and practitioners are to become reflective thinkers within a culture of reflective practice, organizations must provide encouragement, support, feedback, and confidence-building affirmation. A collaboration mindset emphasizes including stakeholders into goal setting, visioning, and clear messaging throughout the organization.

Conclusion

Remember learning to ride a bike? You felt awkward at first. Each time you got back on, you focused on a different tactic all the while trying to stay balanced. You were lifting your feet at different times, trying the brakes at various pressures, and struggling to look where you wanted to go, all the while preoccupied by what your limbs should be doing. Speaker and author Simon Sinek (2017) uses this bike riding analogy as an important factor in our personal motivation: As you attempted to ride, more than likely you fell more than a few times. However, you continued to try until you mastered the art of cycling.

Likewise, building a culture of reflective practice involves learning new skills, balancing pace of development, and remembering that the culture is about the collective "we" and not a singular "I." It is easy to say we are going to change, easy to make preparations; the reality, of course, is that meaningful transformation is rarely quick or easy and realistic expectations are essential to success (Scheffer, Braun, & Scheffer, 2017).

A culture of reflective practice is not a destination; it is a process that is ongoing without an end point. Practitioners experience an action, reflect on the action, use application to associate the action with actual life situations, then use an evaluative process to identify the impact the action has for the future. Building a reflective culture benefits students because it provides an opportunity to review previous actions and results while developing problem-solving skills. Learners accept the concept of questioning the past before moving forward; therefore, encouraging the use of prior experience in future decision-making. Building a culture of reflective practice benefits students by introducing learning skills designed to serve individual learners for life. Instructors using reflective practice provide students with the ability to frame and reframe. The culture must support faculty by encouraging creative design and ensuring that reflective practice can occur in an environment where there are opportunities to learn from others.

Teachers and students must share their experience and be willing to accept the experiences shared in return. For example, a student sitting by a body of water as the sun is setting may reflect upon events from his or her past, perhaps remembering Otis Redding's classic song, Sitting on the Dock of The Bay. The words of the song have little meaning by themselves; they are just lyrics. In isolation, this student just moves on to his/her next thought. Using reflective learning tools, our student may turn to the person next to them and begin a dialogue, sharing the experience while examining how, what, and why questions. To be reflective means to mentally wander through where you have been and to try to make sense of it (Costa & Kallick, 2000). In the next chapter, we will take this self-analysis a step further and consider how reflective practice can be implemented in assessment.

References

Bellot, J. (2011). Defining and assessing organizational culture. *Nursing Forum*, *46*(1), 29–37. doi: 10.1111/j.1744-6198-6198.2010.00207.x.

Brookfield, S. (1987). *Developing critical thinkers: Challenging adults to explore alternative ways of thinking and acting*. San Francisco, CA: Jossey-Bass.

Costa, A. L., & Kallick, B. (2000). Getting into the habit of reflection. *Educational Leadership*, *57*, 60–62

Dewey, J. (1916). *Democracy and education*. New York: The Free Press.

Hall, P., & Simeral, A. (2017). *Creating a culture of reflective practice: Capacity building for schoolwide success*. Alexandria, Egypt. ASCD

Harkness, T., Porter, C., & Hettich, D. (2001). *Articulation and reflection: Emerging perspectives on learning, teaching, and technology*. Retrieved from http://projects.coeuga.edu/epltt/index.php?title=Articulation_and_Reflection

Klemp, G. O., & McClelland, D. C. (1986). What characterizes intelligent functioning among senior managers? In R. J. Steinberg & R. K. Wagner (Eds.), *Practical intelligence: Nature and origins of competence in the everyday world*. Cambridge, England: Cambridge University Press.

Kramsch, C. (1998). *Language and culture*. Oxford, England: Oxford University Press.

Lizzio, A., & Wilson, K. (2004). Action learning in higher education: An investigation of its potential to develop professional capability. *Studies in Higher Education*, *29*(4), 469.

Martin, M. M. (n.d.). *Creating an organizational culture of reflective practice*. Retrieved from https://www.michelemmartin.com/thebambooproject/20008/03/creating-an-org.html

Niculescu, G. (2014). New considerations about action research. *Letter and Social Science Series*, *4*, 28–32.

Reason, P., & Bradbury, H. (Eds.) (2001). *Handbook of action research: Participative inquiry and practice*. London, England: Sage.

Scheffer, A., Braun, N., & Scheffer, M. (2017). *Hanging the mirror: The discipline of reflective leadership*. Minneapolis, MN: Wisdom Editions.

Schein, E. H. (1992). *Organizational culture and leadership*. San Francisco, CA: Jossey-Bass.

Sherwood, G. D., & Horton-Deutsch, S. (2015). *Reflective organizations: On the front lines of QSEN & reflective practice implementations*. Indianapolis, IN: Sigma Theta Tau International.

Sinek, S. (2017). *Find your why: A practical guide for discovering purpose for you and your team*. New York: Penguin Random House.

Singer, S. J., Falwell, A., Gaba, D., Meterko, M., Hartman, C., & Baker, L. (2009). Identifying organizational cultures that promote patient safety. *Healthcare Management Review*, *34*(4), 300–311.

White, K. (2008). Effective critical reflection: Creating a sustainable culture during (and after) initial teacher education. *He Kupu: The Word*, *1*(3) 46–54.

Wolfberg, A., & Dixon, N. M. (2011). Speaking truth to power: Nurturing a reflective culture at the U.S. Defense intelligence agency. *Reflections*, *10*(4), 1–12.

Yajima, K., Yoshihiro, T., Sato, J., Ichimura, R., & Kishimoto, S. (2022). Instructional design for active learning and evaluation implementation. 7th International Conference on Business and Industrial Research (ICBIR 2022), Bangkok, Thailand.

12
REFLECTION AS ASSESSMENT

At the heart of experiential education is the call for both individuals and teams to become collaborative partners in the learning process. Learning occurs in the doing: experience coupled with reflection. This idea of co-production of learning throughout the educational experience is intricately linked to critical thinking, as well. Critical thinking is a centerpiece of experiential engagement, as teachable moments manifest throughout the reflective learning process. Equally important to critical thinking, however, is producing competent, public service leaders who operate within an ethical framework. The undercurrent beneath this construct of critical thinking paired with ethical reasoning is reflective practice and assessment.

In previous chapters, we explored what reflective practice means, the origins of its theoretical roots, and how it might manifest across educational and workplace settings. These earlier discussions laid the foundation for our final two chapters, which will take the discussion a step further by considering how we might evaluate the impact of reflective practice. Assessment is a critical step so that we can more confidently apply reflective practice to our work in the public sector. This chapter, in particular, focuses on a self-assessment model that was initially developed for use in an academic setting.

This chapter will set the stage for reflection as self-assessment by evaluating the aforementioned pilot tool using a Design-Based Implementation Research (DBIR) approach. In an effort to evaluate the learning outcomes tied to experiential education core competencies, the author piloted a self-assessment model within a graduate public administration program over four semesters and presented the findings at a national conference (Pool-Funai, 2019). As we will discuss further, below, a key aspect of DBIR is recognizing the

DOI: 10.4324/9781003270775-17

applicability of a study to new and varied contexts. Put another way, DBIR seeks "... to improve teaching and learning practice, at scale" (Design Based Implementation Research, n.d.) While the pilot study was conducted in an experiential education scenario, the principles may be applied in other disciplines, as well as beyond the classroom setting. This application aspect beyond a classroom setting will carry over to the final chapter, *Reflection as Forethought*. Chapter 13 will shift the evaluation to the professional environment, as we wrap up our discussion with a charge for the reader's own next steps.

Self-assessment in Experiential Learning

The program learning outcome specifically addressed through the pilot study related to graduate students' involvement in the public policy process. Specifically, the designated competency stated that students should, "Participate in and contribute to the public, fiscal, and economic policy process" (Southern Utah University [SUU], n.d.) As one of five core competencies rated by external accreditors, the graduate program selected participation in public policy as the category to assess through a required experiential learning course. The DBIR framework that was used to evaluate the assessment tool is built upon four principles: actionable focus, collaborative design, theoretical underpinning, and sustainability of design, which will be elaborated below. The pilot study concluded with a discussion of key findings and recommendations for further research regarding assessment of experiential learning courses.

The Master of Public Administration (MPA) degree is targeted toward future public service professionals, and as noted above, the self-assessment pilot was carried out with these prospective graduates in mind. The author began the initial DBIR analysis for the purpose of broadening application opportunities for the self-assessment tool to be used in other academic disciplines beyond public service; however, as noted above, the scope of this chapter and the next will explore the use of such an evaluation tool beyond the classroom setting. Following is a brief summary of the four DBIR elements from the pilot study, before we turn our attention to the applicability of a reflective assessment model within the public sector workplace.

Actionable Focus

The premise of the DBIR process is that work should be conducted jointly; it is not a singular effort of an individual. The research centers on the implementation of a design, and input from varied stakeholders is integral to the process. Problem-solving needs to involve dialogue and negotiation across power dynamics, rather than a top-down approach. Peers need to bounce ideas with peers, and organizational leaders need to be open to receiving feedback from subordinates. As problems are identified, action steps should be orchestrated in a manner that leads to positive change not only with regard to the particular design being evaluated but also ultimately to the organization as a whole.

The year that the pilot study took place, the graduate program's accrediting agency announced a new focal point for ethical reasoning skills beyond a singular Ethics course. More specifically, the agency expected programs to intertwine ethics throughout the graduate curriculum. While many MPA programs continued offering an Ethics course through their core or elective curriculum, the accreditor wanted to see evidence that programs were also addressing ethical reasoning skills in other courses, as well. How might a class on public policy development incorporate ethical dilemmas into its discussions? How could we link ethical decision-making to a class on research methods? And, more importantly, how might we assess these efforts?

The MPA program in the pilot study recognized its *Professional Project* experiential learning course as an ideal testing ground to assess students' competencies in navigating ethical dilemmas through traditional written assignments, as well as online discussion prompts and interactive case studies. Another aspect of the external agency's comprehensive review of accreditation standards during this time pertained to producing culturally competent graduates. As we discussed in Chapter 2, reflective administrator is cognizant of how their attitudes and actions impact and influence individuals and processes around them. Culture is a blend of organizational structure, reward, and information systems, the people within the institution or agency, leadership dynamics, and operational processes. Chapter 11 illustrated this notion of organizational culture further by describing it as necessarily engaging in continuous improvement and willingness to change.

The MPA program involved in the pilot study interpreted this expectation of cultural competency as an additional opportunity to evaluate students' critical thinking skills (Association of American Colleges and Universities [AAC&U], n.d.-a). Collectively, the program determined that graduates should be adept problem-solvers with the ability to think critically and make ethical decisions (AAC&U, n.d.-b) within a changing workplace environment, while working productively and effectively with diverse groups and individuals. This initiative dovetailed with another of the program's core competencies: "Communicate orally and in writing in a way that is productive and effective in a diverse and changing workforce and citizenry" (SUU, n.d.).

Student participants in the pilot study courses were given the AAC&U definitions for both *ethical reasoning* and *critical thinking* and asked to gauge their own competency level for each of these skill sets from a Likert scale of four rankings. The AAC&U notes that ethical reasoning "requires students to be able to assess their own ethical values and the social context of problems, recognize ethical issues in a variety of settings, think about how different ethical perspectives might be applied to ethical dilemmas, and consider the ramifications of alternative actions. Students' ethical self-identity evolves as they practice ethical decision-making skills and learn how to describe and analyze positions on ethical issues" (Rhodes, 2010).

However, critical thinking is defined by the AAC&U as "a habit of mind characterized by the comprehensive exploration of issues, ideas, artifacts, and events before accepting or formulating an opinion or conclusion" (Rhodes, 2010). In order to consider ourselves critical thinkers, we need to first understand that what we hold true in our worldview may not be comprehensive to what others around us think (this hearkens back to our discussion from Chapter 7). A critical thinker must recognize that their own perceptions of society and events are largely a product of their own opinions, and acknowledging that others also approach the conversation from their own vantage points will go a long way in helping a reflective administrator to engage in meaningful interactions with colleagues, supervisors, and the general public.

> **MIRROR MOMENT**
>
> How do the AAC&U's definitions above resonate with your understanding of Ethical Reasoning and Critical Thinking? What are some examples of ethical dilemmas that you have experienced or witnessed, either in an educational setting or workplace? What does it mean to you to have "a habit of mind" that explores varied and contrasting ideas?

As part of the self-assessment questionnaire, students were asked to rate themselves on a scale of 1–4 for both skill sets, where 1 = Benchmark; 4 = Mastery. The scales were patterned after the AAC&U's rubrics for each competency. Following are the four options for each criterion:

Rate yourself on your Critical Thinking skills:

1. I take information/viewpoints from experts at face-value, as fact.
2. When I take a stand on an issue, I realize others may have different opinions, but I don't question other viewpoints.
3. I realize that my perspective on certain issues may differ from others' assumptions, and both may be questioned.
4. I develop my viewpoints within context, considering that issues may be complex and seen from varied perspectives.

Rate yourself on your Ethical Reasoning skills:

1. I recognize basic or overt ethical issues but am unable to apply ethical concepts to new scenarios.
2. I am able to state a position and the pros/cons of a particular ethical issue, but I treat each ethical question as a standalone issue.

3. I can spot ethical issues within gray areas, but I don't fully grasp how multiple issues are related to each other.
4. I see the interconnectedness between ethical issues in gray or complex areas, and I am able to defend my position.

Experiential education was already a noted feature within this particular graduate program, so the hands-on *Professional Project* course was a natural starting point for incorporating ethical reasoning and critical thinking components more deliberately into the curriculum, which later formed the basis of the pilot study. The *Professional Project* course is uniquely crafted to each student and is shaped around their own interests and aspirations, as well as the needs of the organization or agency where the project takes place. Examples of students' projects in the *Professional Project* course include things like preparing a Policy & Procedure manual for a department within a government agency; coordinating a volunteer training program for a nonprofit organization; conducting a policy analysis for an agency leading into the legislative session; submitting a new parks and recreation development proposal to a City Council; or, preparing a grant proposal to generate external funding for an institution or organization.

Expectations of the *Professional Project* course include developing a project proposal and also outlining necessary steps the student will take to address a problem, policy, or operational issue within a public agency or nonprofit organization. The proposed project may not necessarily come to fruition within the term of the student's class; however, the student is responsible for laying the groundwork to initiate the endeavor. Therefore, this pilot self-assessment was designed to help students analyze their own performance and/or projects in a manner that incorporates experiential learning theory, critical thinking, and ethical decision-making.

Collaborative Design

DBIR is inherently participatory and should engage multiple stakeholders throughout the process. While curriculum and programming may be natural testing grounds for design improvements in an educational setting, the process should also engage extracurricular aspects such as professional development and related support systems. DBIR is experimental, and as such, the design process may likely be tweaked along the way. This experimentation is a positive part of the process, because the overall system improves as we learn and adapt to challenges, mistakes, and setbacks. As we will see later in this chapter and as we transition to the final chapter, the self-assessment model piloted in this study has evolved and adapted, thanks to input from peer practitioners and scholars, as well as feedback from participants.

In keeping with the expectation to involve a variety of stakeholders in the design process, the blended self-assessment model used in the pilot study was tested in four semesters of the *Professional Project* course and included in the program's accreditation self-study report. Sample narrative feedback from students' self-assessments, as well as initial aggregated results, were included in the accreditation report. Also during the conference where the author shared the framework of the self-assessment pilot, participants had the opportunity to unpack each step of the model through a Design Thinking exercise collectively, discuss and critique the rubric in small groups, and begin drafting their own version of the self-assessment resource that they could take back and implement within their own programs and institutions.

The model became known as *I CARE [to act ethically]*, which was designed as a self-assessment tool to raise ethical awareness and hone critical thinking skills in an experiential learning environment. The acronym stands for: **I**nvolve, **C**onsider, **A**pply, **R**eflect, **E**valuate. Let's break down what each step looks like, in the context of the pilot study:

1. **Involve:** At the beginning of the term, learners selected at least one core competency from a prescribed list of five options that they would focus on for the duration of the *Professional Project* course.
    a. Lead, manage, and apply effective public governance.
    b. Participate in and contribute to the public, fiscal, and economic policy process.
    c. Solve problems using analytics, critical thinking, ethical thinking, and conceptualizing and applying best practices.
    d. Articulate and apply public service perspectives, norms, and legal skills.
    e. Communicate orally and in writing in a way that is productive and effective in a diverse and changing workforce and citizenry (SUU, n.d.).

    Some students took the course over multiple semesters, so this step was highly individualized, based on each student's specific project. (After feedback from the initial pilot study, this step was adapted to a prescribed core competency, which specified students' ability to "lead, manage, and apply effective public governance" so as to consolidate the assessment focus of the *Professional Project* course.)
2. **Consider:** This reflection-on-action step at the end of the project compelled students to describe a scenario where they were able to implement their selected core competency(ies) during the experiential learning course. Students shared anecdotal stories about ways in which they took on a leadership role, incorporated their classroom lessons in the field, and how they made the connection between theory and practice.
3. **Apply:** Students were encouraged to think of instances where they used reflection-in-action skills by identifying challenges that arose during the

course and how they were able to apply public service values in the midst of the difficult experience to address the issues they were facing. Feedback in this area included commentary about times when the students needed to make a change during an experience, coordinate efforts with a supervisor and/or other colleagues, and shift directions on the spot as they worked through a problem.

4. **Reflect:** In this question, students were asked to explain a time when their expectations or assumptions were challenged during the project, or a time when they used critical thinking skills to solve a problem during the course. Answers to this particular question led the researcher to realize that reflection is truly more than just a phase in the learning process; rather, it is intertwined throughout the entire experience. Students' responses to this question illustrated ways in which they put their critical thinking skills to use in order to solve a problem, assist a client, or address a challenge.

5. **Evaluate:** The final step of the self-assessment called on students to use reflection-for-action thinking to identify how the experiential learning course helped to prepare them to be better problem solvers in the future, based on their current profession or future career goals. Students also rated any self-identified improvements in their critical thinking and ethical reasoning skill sets on a sliding scale. This final step in the self-evaluation provided students with an opportunity to think ahead about how they might apply the skills gained in their *Professional Project* course toward their future professional goals.

MIRROR MOMENT

The prompts from the I CARE acronym were disseminated in the context of a graduate-level experiential learning course. However, the principles behind the questions are relevant for a variety of reflective applications. Using your own organization or institution's mission statement, for example, how do you see yourself **involved** in that effort? **Consider** ways that your job supports the overarching mission. How can you **apply** the mission statement more directly in your day-to-day work? **Reflect** on a time when you were challenged by the organization's mission and **evaluate** how your future/ongoing efforts can support the mission statement.

The conference session was crafted to help participants implement a similar self-assessment evaluation using the I CARE framework as a reference, yet with the flexibility to adjust the model to the unique needs and goals of their own programs or institutions. Participants were encouraged to think through the five prompts in the context of their own situations, and the deliverable of the conference session was a sketch of the self-assessment resource with individualized notes for each step.

Theoretical Underpinning

We focused extensively in earlier chapters on foundational theories that guide the implementation of experiential education and reflective practice. Likewise, the DBIR process necessitates that we consider the intersection between theory and practice as a basis for research and the improvement of educational systems. The *I CARE [to act ethically]* model leaned on Kolb's (1984) learning cycle, in addition to critical thinking steps framed by Heinrich, Habron, Johnson, and Goralnik (2015). The framework developed during the pilot study incorporates Kolb's learning cycle: Experience, Reflection, Thinking, and Acting, in addition to five underlying components of critical thinking, which include: analyzing issues, applying evidence, framing the issues, questioning assumptions, as well as identifying relevant solutions. These critical thinking elements will be fleshed out further, below.

As noted in previous chapters, the Kolb cycle is often visualized as a wheel for learners to travel from one phase of learning to the next. The self-assessment model that was developed during the pilot study, however, carries the learner through reflective practice for the duration of the experience, rather than reflection being treated as a standalone step in the process. Reflection is still purposeful, but it is intertwined, not solitary. The imagery here is more of a slinky toy arcing downstairs: the spiral of reflective learning loops over and over itself as each step is implemented (Figure 12.1).

While the experiential learning process is a vital aspect of the *I CARE [to act ethically]* model, another important element centers on five critical thinking principles, which dovetail with the Kolb cycle:

1. Experience
2. Reflection
3. Thinking
4. Acting

Learners begin by *involving* themselves in an experiential learning endeavor – this coincides with Kolb's Experience stage. As noted above, this is also the step in the pilot project where students identify the competency they will be focusing on. For the duration of the experience, they reflectively *consider* the context of their work, as it relates to both theory and practice and subsequently *apply* relevant pieces of their coursework to the experience itself. These two steps are where the students identify scenarios within their *Professional Project* course experience where they engaged in reflective practice. Again, *reflection*

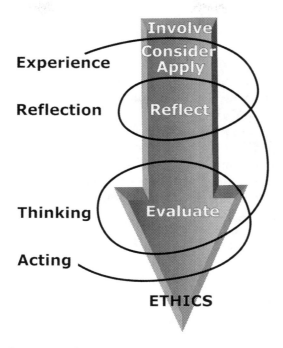

FIGURE 12.1 The *I CARE [to act ethically]* model

is reiterated within the process as a reminder that reflection-on-action, in-action, and for-action are critical aspects of the learning process – the latter being especially valuable as the learner moves into the *evaluate* phase, as they act upon their experience from an ethical framework.

Through the DBIR lens, theory guides both the design and implementation of curriculum, such as the experiential learning tool piloted in this study. The well-known Kolb cycle incorporates reflection as a step in the process of experiential learning, but we are striving to move beyond reflection as a stage and placing it more as an undercurrent. While the new *I CARE [to act ethically]* model proposes a different focus from the traditional Kolb cycle, it retains the overarching goal of improving students' experiences both in the classroom and even beyond their formal studies.

MIRROR MOMENT

How does the *I CARE [to act ethically]* model strike you, with regard to what you have learned so far about reflective practice? Do you see reflection as a stage in the learning process or as an interwoven aspect of the learning cycle? Why or why not?

Sustainability of Design

Lastly, the DBIR process hinges upon a commitment to continuous improvement. Organizations, agencies, and institutions can build capacity for ongoing development by drafting appropriate operations and processes to accommodate changes into their policies and goal planning. In keeping with the spirit of a DBIR framework, the pilot model needed to entail a process that was relevant, adaptable, and sustainable. Relevancy comes into play as we recognize the need to weave ethics throughout the curriculum. Adaptability pertains to students' individualized projects that took place during the pilot study. Sustainability relates to the program's ability to cultivate ethical reasoning and critical thinking skills among its graduates. These are life-long skills that the students will take into their transition to become practitioners in public service.

Case Study

Here, we will recreate the Design Thinking activity that participants completed during the conference presentation, both individually and within small groups. The live session centered on three objectives:

1. Demonstrate an understanding of the Kolb cycle and critical thinking methods, as they relate to experiential learning.
2. Identify the components of the *I CARE [to act ethically]* blended self-assessment model for experiential learning.
3. Draw application of critical thinking to experiential learning within an ethical framework.

After a brief introduction and overview of the ethical reasoning and critical thinking focus areas of the pilot study, the speaker engaged participants in two Design Thinking exercises, where individuals were asked to record ten words or short phrases that come to mind when they think of the term *ethics* in a classroom setting (the second round was *critical thinking*). At the end of the brainstorming time, participants were directed to narrow down their list to the top three and share them with their table. Each table, then, needed to identify the top three words or phrases, collectively, and share them with the large group. The presenter recorded all of the responses, noting any duplications and other similarities.

For the purpose of recreating this exercise for the individual reader, begin by quickly drafting your own list of ten words or phrases that come to mind when you think of *ethics*, either in the context of an educational setting or your workplace. The activity is intended to pull ideas from the top of your head, not to spend time dwelling over your answers, so record your responses as promptly as you can think of them. Set a timer and allow yourself no more than 2–3 minutes for this step.

Next, review your list and narrow it down to your top three words or phrases. Begin to unpack these terms in the context of your educational setting or workplace: What would it look like if your institution, agency, or organization took your three ethical terms to heart and implemented them in a purposeful fashion, even built them into its mission statement and strategic plan? On a smaller scale, what would your own job and interactions with others look like if you and your colleagues (or fellow students) lived out those three ethical concepts on a daily basis? How might your workplace or school evolve?

Repeat the exercise using *critical thinking* as the key term, starting with an off-the-cuff list of ten items, then whittle it down to three. Again, ask the questions at both a micro- (your own experience and interactions) and macro-level (the department or organization, as a whole). What would an institution or organization comprised of critical thinkers do differently than it might be doing currently? How would your own approach to your studies and/or work change, if you embraced your top three critical thinking terms?

Conclusion

The two primary focal points of the *I CARE [to act ethically]* self-assessment model were ethical reasoning and critical thinking skills. While these emphases in the pilot study were fueled by the program's impending reaccreditation – namely, the expectations of the external accreditor to demonstrate an ethical undercurrent throughout the curriculum – the program also wanted to apply the model to evaluate the professional competency of its graduates. The pilot study centered on a graduate program in public administration, but the goal of the *I CARE [to act ethically]* model was adaptation to broader, diverse academic disciplines. In the next and final chapter, we will take this evolving self-assessment tool even further by considering its applicability in the public sector workplace and beyond.

References

Association of American Colleges and Universities (AAC&U). (n.d.-a). Critical thinking VALUE Rubric. Retrieved from https://www.aacu.org/value/rubrics/critical-thinking

Association of American Colleges and Universities (AAC&U). (n.d.-b). Ethical reasoning VALUE Rubric. Retrieved from https://www.aacu.org/ethical-reasoning-value-rubric

Design Based Implementation Research. (n.d.). *Organizing the design process*. Retrieved from http://learndbir.org/principles/organizing-the-design-process

Heinrich, W. F., Habron, G. B., Johnson, H. L., & Goralnik, L. (2015). Critical thinking assessment across four sustainability-related experiential learning settings. *Journal of Experiential Education, 38*(4), 373–393. doi: 10.1177/1053825915592890.

Kolb, D. A. (1984). *Experiential learning: Experience as the source of learning and development*. Englewood Cliffs, NJ: Prentice Hall.

Pool-Funai, A. E. (2019). Assessing critical thinking & ethical reasoning in experiential learning courses. Talk Presented at 2019 National Society for Experiential Education conference, St. Petersburg, FL.

Rhodes, T. (2010). *Assessing outcomes and improving achievement: Tips and tools for using rubrics*. Washington, DC: Association of American Colleges and Universities.

Southern Utah University. (SUU). (n.d.). Master of Public Administration program. Program goals. Retrieved from https://www.suu.edu/hss/polscj/mpa/mission-goals.html

13
REFLECTION AS FORETHOUGHT

To this point, we have explored theories and practice of reflection, learned about tools we can use to become more reflective administrators, and considered pathways to help us implement reflective practice into our own lives and careers. We also looked at ways in which we could use reflection as a medium for organizational change. In this final chapter, we will bring it all full-circle by sharing a Reflective Practice Assessment model that you can put to use toward your own professional development, in a classroom setting, or within your organization.

Evolution of the Reflective Practice Assessment Model

The previous chapter discussed a pilot study in which a self-assessment tool was developed for use in experiential learning settings. With expanded context in mind, the assessment model described below sought to adapt and evolve the *I CARE [to act ethically]* pilot from simply a learning tool into a design more suitable for broad application by practitioners. An overarching goal of both the pilot tool, as well as the new model we will discuss in this chapter, is to embrace a trajectory of continuous improvement within public service professions through reflective self-assessment. The notion of quality improvement is deeply seeded in the private sector, and educational systems make heavy use of assessment, but these practices have not yet taken hold across the public sector, at large. Through the Reflective Practice Assessment model, we hope to change that trend going forward.

Both students and public sector administrators can benefit from quality improvement tools that have historically been associated primarily with the business community, yet with a deliberate focus on the unique missions of public service agencies. The Reflective Practice Assessment model described below connects students and practitioners through a cycle of lifelong learning, so that future generations of public leaders can truly be reflective administrators who are empowered with critical thinking and ethical reasoning skills.

Knowing where to begin a reflective practice assessment is often a difficult step. When we, as public service leaders and lifelong learners, attempt to use standard assessment models that do not account for reflection-in action, reflection-on-action and reflection-for-action, then we do ourselves (and our organizations) a disservice by not engaging in a progressive assessment process that ensures the outcomes/results are authentic and realistic for continuous improvement. The Reflective Practice Assessment model presented here seeks to bridge this gap by weaving reflection throughout the evaluation process.

Reflective Practice Assessment Model as Seen through a Design-Based Implementation Research (DBIR) Lens

Using a similar approach as introduced in Chapter 12, we will explore the Reflective Practice Assessment model through a Design-Based Implementation Research (DBIR) lens by discussing its actionable focus, collaborative design, theoretical underpinning, and sustainability of design. The chapter will conclude with a call to action, as the reader identifies opportunities for implementation within their own institution, organization, or agency (Figure 13.1).

Actionable Focus

The Reflective Practice Assessment model was designed to raise ethical awareness and hone critical thinking skills within a reflective practice environment. Assessment of reflective practice within an educational setting can take place in a variety of venues, such as an internship, departmental project, policy analysis, or other professional experience. In a professional setting, however, opportunities to engage in reflective practice will likely be more organic and less structured. The Reflective Practice Assessment model can guide us through purposeful, action-oriented reflection, regardless of the level of formality involved in the experience.

We will go through each component of the model in more detail in the next section, but the actionable focus of the design is its three-part reflection phases. As we have discussed throughout the text, reflective practice can manifest in the moment (in-action), in hindsight (on-action), and as a tool for next steps (for-action). This traid works in sync with each step, as the learner progresses through the reflective practice cycle.

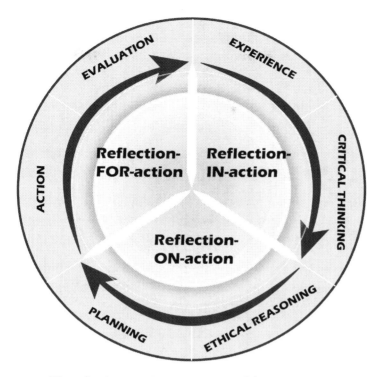

FIGURE 13.1 The reflective practice assessment model

Collaborative Design

We started our discussion of the DBIR framework in Chapter 12 by explaining that "the aim of design is to improve teaching and learning practice, at scale" (LearnDBIR, n.d.). The new Reflective Practice Assessment model came to life as the authors began to examine how the *I CARE [to act ethically]* pilot study might evolve beyond a limited educational setting and apply more effectively to the broader public sector workplace. The authors sought to mesh established theories related to experiential learning, best practices for reflective thought, and necessary professional skills of ethical reasoning and critical thinking into a collective, cyclical framework. The resulting Reflective Practice Assessment model features six elements paired into three phases that build upon each other and guide the user to engage in a reflective review of the learning experience to aid individual, departmental, and – ultimately – organizational improvement.

Reflection-in-Action

The reflective process begins with in-action, which could entail scenarios such as the moment(s) during a meeting, a presentation, or conversation when thoughts are improvisational and problems are solved rapidly. As demonstrated in Chapter 3, professionals use reflection-in-action to identify perceived problems in the moment as well as thinking while doing. The text refers to action that is taking place in real time with an opportunity to step back for review. Reflection-in-action happens during a snapshot in time without allowance for processing that is more readily available in the on-action and for-action stages. As stated in Chapter 4, practitioners become critically aware of assumptions made by themselves and others during this phase. Reflection-in-action incorporates experience and critical thinking as the key elements before practitioners move on to the next phase of the reflective process.

1. **Experience** is what practitioners bring to the table, based on their own knowledge, practice, and exposure. Experience is the initial contribution practitioners provide to an individual or group problem-solving session. It is the guide for collective and individual thought on a topic or process. In Chapter 5, Kolb's experiential learning theory was presented as a functional part of reflective practice, which centers on experience at its core.
2. **Critical Thinking** requires practitioners to step back so they may review and assess as a process or activity continues. Operating in a reflective dimension requires practitioners to internally examine and explore memories, actions, and perspectives that are activated by experiences for clarification and meaning. As Chapter 8 reminded us, these important critical thinking skills can guide us to review assumptions and question the norms that could lead to change.

Reflection-on-Action

Previous chapters consistently reinforced that learning does not occur by accident. Reflection-on-action takes place when practitioners integrate their accumulated professional knowledge to implement possible alternatives for resolving a concern or issues. As an analytical process, this form of reflection offers perspective for new understandings, beliefs, and values. Ethical reasoning and planning both come into play during this phase of the cycle. Chapter 3 reminded us that while this step involves hindsight, it is also a forward-thinking effort that leads to the final stage of reflective practice (reflection-for-action).

1. **Ethical Reasoning** comes to light because practitioners and leaders are often confronted with decision-making tasks that can be the final approval or denial of a project, policy, or action. Reflection-on-action involves a process of reviewing weaknesses and strengths, as well as negative interpersonal influences like self-justification, biased behavior, self-appreciation, and deception. As we learned in Chapter 7, recognizing

that each of us possesses implicit biases to one extent or another is critical to overcoming these hurdles. Such issues must be addressed prior to a final decision or presentation to a group for the development of outcomes. The expectation of ethical reasoning is for teams and individual participants to demonstrate mindfulness (Chapter 5), good practice (Chapter 3), and hindsight (Chapter 4), so reflective administrators can interact with integrity and honesty. Ethical reasoning is hard work; while striving to achieve it, one must remain willing to combat egocentric tendencies of an individual (including themselves) or group that may be working against fair and equitable growth.
2. **Planning** is necessary in order for us to move from reflection-on-action to reflection-for-action. This process involves collecting ideas from one or more individuals, and planning is a direct outcome of notations and ideas that were reviewed and discussed during reflection-on-action sessions. Planning consists of interaction, dynamic elements, and decision points; it is a fluid process that requires flexibility for change en route. Practitioners addressing planning can examine ideas sequentially or simultaneously. The objective is to arrange and identify questions, situations, objectives, and potential outcomes for additional review and development within reflection- for-action.

Reflection-for-Action

The final pairing of the Reflective Practice Assessment model incorporates prior experience and thinking beyond what is currently in place. Reflection-for-action calls for us to anticipate the need for actions that can correct problems, address challenging issues, and facilitate process improvements. The concern here is about what can be done to improve current shortfalls in the future through a deliberate evaluation process. Chapters 3, 10, and 11 provided an overview of the elements helpful in moving a team, organization, or educational institution toward potential improvements using reflection-for-action.

1. **Action** as a step in the reflective practice process is not movement simply for action's sake. It involves an examination of ideas, values, beliefs, practices, and theories. Action research is often used to collect data; Chapter 6 describes action research as the work or engagement that occurs within a state of action. It engages practitioners both within their individual environments and within the organization at large. Action research performs best in association with other practitioners and requires communication among participants to share and shape research questions and design.
2. **Evaluation** is a dynamic and ongoing process. Evaluation is a product of critical thinking that promotes distinct transitions between problem identification, diagnosis, exploration, and action that are often difficult

to discern. It is important to take time to critically reflect or take stock of data provided as a result of an evaluation. Practitioners are then able to make judgments about the effectiveness of prior actions or engagements that can lead to process improvements to correct past errors.

Collectively, the three types of reflective practice joined with pairs of affiliated steps point us toward a comprehensive cycle of Reflective Practice Assessment that can be implemented in educational, workplace, and professional development contexts.

Theoretical Underpinning

Each step of the Reflective Practice Assessment model focuses on the intersection of theory and practice, with a keen emphasis on application. The assessment process hinges on providing interactive practice opportunities during each phase for learners to engage other colleagues or fellow students within practical and authentic settings. The triad of reflective practice stages stems from early research on reflection, including the likes of Dewey and Kolb described in Chapter 1. Kolb and Kolb's (2005) four-part cycle includes steps of concrete experience, reflective observation, abstract conceptualization, and active experimentation, which helped to inform the redesigned six stages of the new Reflective Practice Assessment model: experience, critical thinking, ethical reasoning, planning, action, and evaluation.

Critical thinking and ethical reasoning were added to the mix as a direct result of the pilot study described in Chapter 11. These two integral skills were identified as important tools for public sector leaders to hone, as well as key components of the reflective practice process. The pilot study, *I CARE [to act ethically]*, began as a self-assessment tool to raise ethical awareness and hone critical thinking skills in the context of an experiential education environment, and the acronym broke down five phases of the learning process: **I**nvolve, **C**onsider, **A**pply, **R**eflect, **E**valuate. In one way or another, these phases are embedded into the new Reflective Practice Assessment model, though the structure has morphed from a spiral design to the overlapping wheel imagery described above. *Involve* is folded into the *experience* stage; *consider* is part of both *critical thinking* and *ethical reasoning*; *apply* is mirrored in *planning* and *action*; *reflection* is woven throughout the entire cycle; and, *evaluate/ evaluation* remains as the final step of the assessment process.

Sustainability of Design

The reenvisioned Reflective Practice Assessment model presented here focuses on six key phases of assessment and how to utilize each step, as outlined in the Collaborative Design section, above. It bears repeating that assessment is not a one-and-done activity, however. According to Suskie (2009, p. 4), assessment is the ongoing process of:

1. Establishing clear, measurable expectations and outcomes;
2. Ensuring individuals have opportunities to achieve expected outcomes;
3. Systematically gathering, analyzing, and interpreting evidence to determine how results match expectation; and,
4. Using the resulting information to understand and improve process and quality.

Taking each of these benchmarks in turn, we can ensure that the Reflective Practice Assessment model is a sustainable tool for use in a classroom setting and/or professional environment. The six stages are defined and measurable. The three reflection phases encourage participants to continue navigating the cycle as they successfully progress through each step. The evaluation stage is not merely an end goal of data gathering; rather, it is a jumping-off point for a new cycle of reflective practice and learning as the participant applies what they have learned toward a new experience.

Conclusion and Call to Action

As you begin to consider how you might incorporate the Reflective Practice Assessment model into your own educational, workplace, or professional development journey, let's break down each phase in accordance with Suskie's (2009) recommendations mentioned above:

1. *Goals and outcomes.* Not every experience will necessarily begin with clearly articulated outcome expectations; however, as the experience unfolds, we can use critical thinking skills through reflection-in-action to establish our own goals.
2. *Individual opportunity.* By engaging ethical reasoning skills through reflection-on-action and making use of planning, we can ensure that individual and group participants in the experience are poised for success.
3. *Evidence and results.* Remember that action for action's sake is not the goal, but as we use reflection-for action, we can identify how the experience lines up with earlier expectations.
4. *Ongoing improvement.* Lastly, as we evaluate the present experience, we set ourselves up for brand new experiences in the future where we can apply the lessons learned and skills acquired to a new context.

A reflective administrator does not view reflective practice as a standalone endeavor or to-do list; rather, reflection becomes ingrained in their daily lives. Our goal throughout this text, and particularly within this final chapter, has been to prepare the reader for their next experience to apply the knowledge gleaned here and personalize it for their professional growth, with the ultimate hope that each of us will positively impact our own organizations, institutions, and communities, at large.

References

Kolb, A. Y., & Kolb, D. A. (2005 June). Learning styles and learning spaces: Enhancing experiential learning in higher education. *Academy of Management Learning & Education*, 4(2), 193–212. Retrieved from http://www.jstor.org/stable/40214287

LearnDBIR. (n.d.). *Design based implementation research*. Retrieved from http://learndbir.org

Suskie, L. (2009). *Assessing student learning: A common sense guide*. San Francisco, CA: John Wiley & Sons.

INDEX

Note: Page numbers in *italics* refer to figures

Aalsburg Wiessner, C. 44
abstract conceptualization 13, 61, 168
academic advisor 26
action research process: adult learning theory 68; back drop 69; college readmission policy 69; common action 70; nucleus of 69; objective 70; outcomes 70; research practice 70
activities, values, beliefs, and outcomes 55
adaptive leadership 81–83
alienation 65, 115, 128
Allen, K. L. 113, 114
The American Psychological Association 26
andragogy 14–15
appreciative inquiry 42, 44, 76, 79, 128–129, 148
Ash, S. L. 11, 37

Baizhanov, S. 34–39, 41
Baxter Magolda, M. B. 17, 18
Beck, M. 24
black-and-white view 10
Bloom's taxonomy 1, *2*
Bolton, G. 98
Boud, D. 50, 55
Bowman, J. 24
Brookfield, D. S. 15
Brookfield, S. D. 102, 105, 117, 120

Brown, K. W. 63
burnout: motivation forms 126; principal determinant of 126; public service profession 133–135; recognizable phase 128; signs 128

Cady, J. M. 120
Carr, W. 68
case study: culture of reflection 147–148; leadership 83–84; mindfulness 70; pathways of reflection 122; public service profession 133–135; public service values 31; reflection as hindsight 58; reflection of good practice 42–43; reflection of theory 18–19; resilient organizations 98–99; self analysis reflection 110; self-assessment evaluation 160–161
Chapin, R. K. 27
Cheng, Y. 129
Clayton, P. H. 11, 37
cognitive reflective process 56
collaborative reflection 57
Collective memory 62
collective reflection 55, 56
communication 15, 16, 21, 24–26, 30, 35, 63, 69, 76, 82, 84, 85, 95, 107, 119, 141, 142, 145, 147, 167
community stakeholders 42–44, 53, 58, 70, 71, 84, 140, 147, 148

Congressional Research Service 10
constructive reflection 55
Costa, A. L. 146
Coulson, D. 38
COVID-19 pandemic 98, 99, 126
Creswell, J. D. 63
critical reflection: challenging reflection 42; connected reflection 41; contextualized reflection 42; continuous reflection 41; professional experience 41
critical thinking 5, 16, 40, 42, 52, 55, 61, 89, 105, 115, 120, 139, 145, 151, 153–158, 160, 161, 164–169
cultural competency 24, 26, 27, 153
culture of reflection: action research 143; classroom environment 139; communication 142; complicated process 141; creation 143–147, *144*; language 147; reflective practice 139–141; shared mental models 142

Davis, J. D. 66, 68
Davis, T. 107
Dehler, G. 105
Descartes, R. 89
Design-Based Implementation Research (DBIR) approach 5, 151, 152, 155, 158–160. *see also* Reflective Practice Assessment model, DBIR lens
destructive leadership 4, 80–81
Dewey, J. 1, 4, 12, 90–92, 139
Dixon, N. M. 143

Eberhardt, J. L. 28, 29
emotional complexity 56–58
emotional labor 126
empowering leadership 75–76
empowerment evaluation 106–108
epochal transformation 53
exhaustion 128
experiential learning reflections: bridging learning and practice *118*, 118–120; classroom creation 120–122; reflective practice 115–118; workforce preparation 114–115
experiential learning theory 12–14, 50, 61, 62, 82, 155, 166
Eyler, J. 40–42

Federal Communications Commission (FCC) 24
Fenwick, T. J. 116

Fetterman, D. M. 107
Fogarty, R. J. 17, 38
Foley, G. 113
Freeman, L. C. 26

Gallagher, T. 13
Germundsen, R. A. 120
Giles, D. E. 40–42
Golden Rule 90–92, 96; economic axiom 92; inverse interpretation 91–92; philosophical stature 90; preemptive justification 92; resilient organization 93–95, *94*; standard version 90–91; universal truth 89, 90, 96
González Sullivan, L. 44
Goralnik, L. 158
Graduate Teaching Assistants (GTAs) 83
Grashow, A. 34
Greeny, J. 105
Guthrie, L. K. 49, 54
Guy, M. E. 10, 11

Habron, G. B. 158
Hall, P. 145
Hamilton, A. 9
Harkness, T. 146
Harvey, M. 38
Heifetz, R. A. 34, 81, 82
Heinrich, W. F. 158
Hettich, D. 146
Hilden, S. 57
Holton, E., III 15
Horton-Deutsch, S. 35, 52, 148
How We Think (Dewey) 1

I CARE model 156–161, *159*, 163, 165, 168
International Association of Chiefs of Police (IACP) 22, 23

Johnson, E. 80, 81
Johnson, H. L. 158
Jones Medine, C. M. 65

Kabat-Zinn, J. 59
Kahneman, D. 80
Kallick, B. 146
Kam, P. K. 130–132
Kegan, R. 13
Kemmis, S. 68
Keogh, D. 50
Khan, J. 96

Kim, J. 126
Kings, R. 64
Klemp, G. O. 144
Knowles, M. 15
Kolb, A. Y. 12, 13, 61, 62, 168
Kolb, D. A. 12, 13, 61, 129, 158–160, 168
Kolb's experiential learning theory 13, 61, 62, 166
Kozmetsky, G. 73
Kramsch, C. 147

Ladegaard Bro, L. 53
leadership: action learning 77–80, 79; adaptive leadership 82, 83; change leadership 76–77; destructive leadership 80–81; empowering leadership 75–76; management to 73–75; mindfulness 67; passive-avoidant leadership 81; transactional leadership 80; transformational leadership 80, 81; transparency 76
lifelong learning 49–51, 55, 164
linguistic competence 27
Linsky, M. 34
Lipsky, M. 29, 30
Liu, H.-C. 129

Maxwell, J. C. 73
McCandless, S. A. 10, 11
McClelland, D. C. 144
McDonald, J. 97
McIver, S. 128
McMillan, R. 105
Merriam, B. S. 13–16
Mezirow, J. 14, 53
mindfulness: actions of 60; benefits 63; creativity 65–66; definition of 60; experiential learning theory 61; leadership development 67; practice of 61; in the real world 66–67; reflective practice 63; theoretical/cultural background 64–65; unbiased awareness 63; in the workplace 67–70
Moriah, J. 25
motivation 25, 57, 76, 81, 126, 130, 135

NASPAA (Network of Schools of Public Policy, Affairs, and Administration) 21, 22, 30, 35
Niculescu, G. 143

Obama, B. 53
O'Brien, R. F. 129, 130

Olteanu, C. 38
Open Government Directive 3, 24, 76, 77

participation and power dynamics: feeling valued 130; identifying service users' strengths 130; interpersonal level 131; learning opportunities 131; public sector workforce 132–133; relationships 131; self-care 130; structural empowerment 132
passive-avoidant leadership 80, 81
pathways of reflection: doubt 4; preparation 4; second wind 4–5; self-analysis 4
Patterson, K. 105
Pearson, T. A. 29
Pete, B. M. 17, 38
Poehler, A. 99
Police Chief Magazine 23
Porter, C. 146
professional competency 24, 26, 31, 82, 161
professional project course 155–158
Progressive reform movement 10
public administration context 39
public sector perceptions 125–126
public service values: accountability and transparency 22–24; competency 24–27; curriculum and beyond 34–35; efficiency 27–28; NASPAA 21, 22, 30; objectivity 28–29; reflective approach 31; respect, equity, and fairness 30; Strengths Perspective 27–28; upholding the public trust 29–30

Qutoshi, B. S. 52

Rapp, C. A. 101, 107
Redding, O. 149
reduced performance 128
reflection as practice in public sector 9–11, 40
reflection-for-action 3, 11, 12, 26, 30–32, 35, 37–40, 42, 44, 55, 57, 62, 66, 78, 79, 81, 97, 108, 128, 131, 143, 147, 148, 157, 164, 166; action 167; evaluation 167–168
reflection for organizational change: assessment 5; forethought 5–6; reflective culture 5

reflection-in-action 3, 11, 12, 23, 30, 35–37, 39–41, 43, 50, 51, 55, 61–63, 66, 77, 79, 83, 91, 108, 115, 121, 127, 128, 143, 147, 148, 156, 169; critical thinking 166; experience 166
reflection-on-action 3, 11, 12, 18, 30, 35, 37, 39–42, 49, 55, 57, 62, 65, 66, 78, 79, 81, 108, 115, 121, 128, 147, 148, 156, 159, 164, 169; ethical reasoning 166–167; planning 167
reflective learning 113–116, 118–120, 122, 142, 145, 149, 151, 158
reflective practice: activation stage 39; active learning through personal relationships 15–17; andragogy 14–15; balancing theory and practice *54*; classroom creativity 120–122; critical thinking skills 16, *17*; experiential learning courses 115–118; experiential learning theory 12–13; identification stage 36–37; integration step 37–38; learning partnership model 17–18; learning process 11; mindfulness 64; public sector professions 125–126; stories 97–98; transformative learning 13–14; types of *36*
Reflective Practice Assessment model, DBIR lens *165*; actionable focus 164; collaborative design 165–168; evidence and results 169; evolution of 163–164; goals and outcomes 169; individual opportunity 169; ongoing improvement 169; sustainability of design 168–169; theory and practice 168
The Reflective Practitioner (Schön) 1
resilient organization 93–95, *94*, 98
richness of reflection 54
Riley, T. D. 64, 67
Robb, D. 93–95, 98
Roff, S. 108, 109
Rosser, C. 9
Ruefli, T. 73
Ryan, R. M. 63

Sager, F. 9
Saleebey, D. 28, 102–104, 106, 108
scaffolding 13, 97, 142, 146
Schaak, D. 120
Schein, E. 25
Schein, E. H. 140
Schmiede, A. 40–42
Schön, D. 1, 35

Schön, D. A. 114, 115
Schuller, R. H. 61
self-assessment evaluation: collaborative design 155–158; critical thinking skills 154; DBIR approach 151, 152, 155, 158–160; ethical reasoning skills 154–155; experiential education 155; experiential learning 152–155; *I CARE* model 158–159, *159*; *professional project* course 155, 156; sustainability of design 160
shared learning process 56
Sherwood, D. G. 52
Sherwood, G. D. 35, 148
Silver Rule 91
Simeral, A. 145
Sinek, S. 149
strength perspective 101–103, *103*; catalyst for change 108–110; elements of strengths 103–105; empowerment evaluation 106–108; language of critique 105–106
Strengths Perspective 27–28
Suskie, L. 169
Svara, J. H. 34–39, 41
Swanson, R. 15
Switzler, R. 105
Sze Goh, A. Y. 55

Tamanaha, B. Z. 90
teaching tool 1
theory and practice of reflection: good practice 3; public service value 2–3; theory 2
Thomas Bernard, W. 25
Thy Jensen, U. 53
Tikkamäki, K. 57
Tisdell, J. E. 64, 67
tools for reflection: hindsight 3; mindfulness 3; perspectives 3–4
Torres, M. 49, 54
transactional leadership 80, 81
transformational leadership 80, 81
transformational power 51–54
Triolo, P. 25
Turesky, F. 13

van der Voet, J. 76, 77
Vella, E. 128
Volpe-White, M. J. 49, 54

Walker, D. 50
Wambach, A. 131

Wardropper, E. 64
Warhurst, R. 116
Weber, M. 9, 10
Weick, A. 101, 102
Welsh, M. 105
West, J. 24
Wheatley, J. M. 66

Wilson, W. 9, 10
Winters, M.-F. 24
Wlodkowski, J. R. 57
Wolfberg, A. 143
workplace, reflective practice 68–70

Zacher, H. 80, 81

Printed in the United States
by Baker & Taylor Publisher Services